# WHO'S MIGUEL?

## GINNY SATTERWHITE

*There is nothing lonelier than a boy who has been loved unconditionally and then abandoned.*

Remember the Chatbas —
Ginny Satterwhite

i

.

For Eloise and Clara

This book is a work of historical- fiction. The events at Jamestowne were researched from the diary of Captain John Smith, Commander of the Susan Constant, and are considered factual.

1. Grieving the death of a parent—Fiction. 2. City of St. Wigbod—Fiction. 3. Time travel.—Fiction 4. Polydactyl cats.—True 5. Powhatan Nation.— True 6. Miscarriage. —Fiction 7. Webbe Memorial Hospital. —Fiction

2. Themes: ( New student at school; loneliness), (Suicide), (Cruelty of cliques), (Friendship), Perseverance), (Forgiveness),(Bullying), (Racial prejudice), (demeaning teachers), (Man's inhumanity to man)

Original *Rampage*

# PROLOGUE

As I was leaving the hospital on that crisp autumn night, I had no idea what was in store for me. I shivered, thinking about the first freeze that would be coming soon. I just wanted to get home and warm up by the fireplace.

I hurried to my 'Doctor's Only' parking space, fished for my keys, and pushed the clicker. My new black and silver Camaro started up and idled smoothly. Just as I reached to open the door I heard something— a cry. I stopped. The sound was coming from the bushes behind the car. I hesitated. Again, I heard it—a wheeze of a cry — and so I decided to investigate. There underneath a holly bush, two small, yellow eyes stared at me. "What in tarnation?"

I reached into the bush, felt the prick of thorns, and grabbed the tiny shivering animal and pulled it out. "Why look at you. What are you doing in there?" When I brushed off the leaves, I discovered a matted, and wet, black kitten, no bigger than my hand. It attempted a feeble hiss. It was weak and scared. I whispered, "Calm down. It's all right. You're safe. Let's warm you up."

I cradled the kitten in the crook of my arm and popped the trunk. I took out a towel, swaddled the kitten and eased into the car. As I was drying it off and cleaning its paws, I noticed it had seven toes on each paw. "I can't believe it! You're a Hemingway! I'm taking you home."

Wrapped in the towel, the shivering soon stopped and the kitten relaxed; he closed his eyes and began to purr.

At home, I bathed him and gave him a saucer of warm milk. As I watched the tiny mouser, a strange sensation came over me. Memories long forgotten, awakened in me and became fresh and new. *Has it really been fifty years?*

I walked over to the hall table and picked up the Wiggins Preparatory invitation I had been ignoring for days. It was a *Save the Date* for the 50th reunion of the Wiggins Preparatory School's class of 1962. I had been dreading this event. After all, I had never gone to one.

Just the thought of Wiggins raised my blood pressure. *It's a miracle I survived. What a confused kid I was.*

I built a fire, picked up the kitten, and settled into my favorite recliner. "I think I'll name you Boots after the Hemingway cat I had when I was a kid." As I rubbed Boots under the chin, I thought about the adventure I had

.

on the *Susan Constant*, heading for Jamestowne, when I found my first Hemingway. *What a trip that was.*

The fire crackled and popped as I stared into its hypnotic light. My mind drifted back though the years and the story unfolded.

.

# CHAPTER 1
# THE ACCIDENT

It was nearly midnight. He remembered the ambulance screeching to a stop on the emergency room driveway of Webbe Memorial. Swarms of medics descended, whisked him from the ambulance, onto a gurney and through swinging hospital doors. He heard cries and moans. *"What's happened? Where's Mama?"* he thought. Then— Darkness. Silence.

******

"Francis?" Someone was shaking his shoulder. "Can you hear me?" A terse voice beckoned through his foggy mind. "It's your grandmother."

*Grandmother? I don't have a grandmother.* His thoughts were hazy, dreamlike.

More poking and prodding, and that was all he remembered.

"Is he in pain?"

"He probably is now," the doctor said. "Your grandson has quite an injury. He has a concussion but I'm confident he will regain consciousness before too long and we can assess his condition better at that point."

Adele Webbe fidgeted with her collar. "Oh, dear me. Will he be all right? You know... *mentally?*"

"Again, we'll assess his condition once he regains consciousness." Dr. Throgmorton checked Freddy's chart and made notations. "Most likely Francis will experience a serious headache for a day or two but he's a healthy 13-year-old and he has youth on his side. Head injuries can result in permanent mental and physical disability, but that's rare."

"Mental and physical disability"? Adele looked distraught. "I overheard a nurse saying there could be amnesia or memory loss." She dabbed at her eyes with a handkerchief. "And that his mother may never recover."

"Let's not jump to conclusions. We simply do not know." Dr. Throgmorton paused. "I'm so sorry, Adele. I know you're worried. Hannah's injuries are serious but your grandson is already showing significant improvement. Let's wait and see."

Dr. Throgmorton dug into his pocket and pulled out a foil wrapped candy. "Adele, I highly recommend these." He opened the *CarPop* wrapper, took Mrs. Webbe's gloved hand, and placed the miniature car-shaped lollipop inside. "Look! It's a 49 Ford. Remember? They were always breaking down." He rested his hand on her shoulder.

A faint smile creased her mouth. "I remember yours. What fun we had."

Adele fidgeted with the candy as she gazed upon the motionless boy. "I just don't know what I'll do. What if he's not right and ends up a vegetable? I have our family name to think about."

Dr. Throgmorton recoiled in disbelief. "Your first concern should be to hope your grandson has a complete recovery. He will need care once he leaves the hospital. Who's going to take care of him as he recovers?"

"I hear there are many excellent military schools back east. I don't know a thing about boys," she said, turning the candy. "I have priceless antiques…. I simply can't have some boisterous person upsetting things."

"You're his next of kin," Dr. Throgmorton said intensely and held her gaze. "I trust you recognize that with his mother in a coma, —she's your daughter, Adele— the boy needs your help if he is to heal properly."

"Yes, of course. I suppose he can stay at Eagles' Nest until more suitable arrangements are made." Mrs. Webbe began to pace. "Still, this might be difficult. You know Hannah and I have been estranged for the past 13 years." She stopped at the window and looked at the full moon. "Francis was just a baby when she left." Mrs. Webbe's eyes welled up. "Things were different back then. I had no choice. What else could I have done? She said she never wanted to see me again. I don't want to ignore her wishes."

"Adele, even though these are horrible circumstances, I'd think you'd be overjoyed to see your family again. Who knows, you might even enjoy having your grandson with you." Dr. Throgmorton shook his head and left the room.

Mrs. Webbe settled into the green hospital chair next to her grandson, put the cherry flavored candy in her mouth. *I don't know if I can stand to have a smelly teenager in my house.*

## CHAPTER 2
## GRANDMOTHER WEBBE

The next morning, Freddy awoke to a pounding above his left eye. He blinked against the bright light and the pain spread around his skull to his right ear. His vision was blurry and he sensed someone near.

"Francis, are you awake?" a woman said.

He tried to focus on the person in front of him. She was peering intently into his blinking eyes.

"Can you see me?" She snapped her fingers above his eyes; the sound reverberated in his head. "Can you talk? Count to ten." She enunciated slowly. "Do—you—understand—me?" She was hovering too close. Freddy felt as if he were prey.

He lay silent trying to make sense of what he heard. The woman sighed and he caught the faint scent of roses.

He felt her tuck the sheet under the mattress and rearrange the blanket at the foot of the bed.

She moved to the sink, lathered, rinsed, and dried her hands. She gazed at her long, red fingernails and Freddy noticed a large diamond ring on her hand.

Freddy tried to speak. His lips were cracked and dry.

The woman turned to look at Freddy. "I'm your grandmother." She walked to the foot of the bed. "You and your mother were in an unfortunate accident on the way to Hickory Creek. It's simply a miracle you survived. Now let's see how you're doing. Can you move your fingers? Your toes?" She reached for his foot and squeezed.

Freddy winced. He had no idea what she was talking about or who this woman was. He struggled to speak, "Where am I? Where's my mother?" Freddy tried to roll over but became tangled up in the IV line.

"You've—been—in—an—accident," she said. "You're in the hospital." She gazed into space as if she was recollecting the events.

"An ambulance took you to the nearest hospital but your mother's injuries were too severe for that *second rate* place, so they brought you both to our hospital here in St. Wigbod. Webbe Memorial is the best."

She looked back at Freddy and smoothed out the kink in the IV line, pulled the top sheet up under his arms, and pinched Freddy's ear. "Your mother is just down the hall," she added. "She'll be fine. Now let's have a look at you. Is your brain working, Francis?"

"My name is Freddy," he said before drifting off to sleep.

Mrs. Webbe drummed her fingernails and repeatedly pressed the call button on the wall above Freddy's bed.

"You certainly took long enough." She said when a voice answered over the static of the intercom. "Adele Webbe here. Tell Dr. Throgmorton I need to see him immediately!"

"Yes, Mrs. Webbe, I'll try to reach him."

"You'd best do better than try," she said. "I'm a founding member of the St. Wigbod Company of the Jamestowne Society and I'm on the board of this hospital," she told the nurse. "What's your name?"

Silence.

The door to Freddy's hospital room flew open and in stormed Dr. Throgmorton. "How dare you speak to my staff with such condescension, Adele! You should be kissing the hands of those caring for your grandson instead

.

of issuing edicts.  One of these days – What did you want, anyway?"

Adele walked over to him and brushed some lint off his shoulder.  "I was just so thrilled about Francis. He was speaking quite coherently before going back to sleep.

Although he doesn't want to answer my questions, it seems his brain is working just fine. Wouldn't you agree?"

"Whatever you say." Dr. Throgmorton turned away. "Yes, he is recovering quite nicely, which I'm sure you're relieved to know."

She smiled and clasped her hands together. "So, no brain damage?"

Dr. Throgmorton shook his head slowly. "No, Adele, but I do have concerns about Hannah."

"Yes, I was just thinking of dear Hannah lying in her room unconscious, alone, unable to do anything for herself." Adele gazed at the flower painting across the room and put her manicured hand to her neck. "She doesn't have any insurance, you know—her treatment will be horrendously expensive. Perhaps it would be better to transfer her to the County Hospital. After all, it is closer to her home. Will you arrange it?"

She saw the disgust on his face. "This is unfathomable, Adele." Dr. Throgmorton spit his words out. "She doesn't need to be close to her home; she needs to be close to you and her son! You know very well that this facility far exceeds County. She's thirty-two years old— she needs her mother, and the very best hospital. Hannah should stay here."

.

Adele pursed her lips and took hold of the doctor's hand. "I'm asking this one favor, Kellam. Do it for me."

# CHAPTER 3
## EAGLES' NEST

Seven days later Freddy was well enough to go home. However, he had no idea where that might be. His mother, Hannah Griswold, in a coma, and showing no signs of recovering, had been transferred to Bruster County Hospital, twenty-five miles from St. Wigbod.

At precisely 7:15 in the morning, Grandmother Webbe strutted into Freddy's room wearing a bright yellow summer frock featuring tropical fruit designs. Atop her head was an oversized, floppy hat decorated with silk grapes, lemons, and cherries. On the brim, an ornamental macaw perched precariously; her dyed red hair peeked out. Crocheted yellow gloves clutched a matching straw purse. She crossed the room and pulled open the curtains; the room filled with sunshine.

"Time to wake up and get dressed, Francis. Put on that outfit I bought for you." She added, "It cost me a pretty penny." She pointed to khaki pants and a checkered shirt draped over the corner chair. "Dr. Throgmorton said you're well enough and so I'm taking you to Eagle's Nest."

Freddy managed to whisper, "Where's my Mom?"

Mrs. Webbe removed her gloves. "You've forgotten again, haven't you?"

"I guess so."

She sighed. "Okay, I'll tell you again. Use those big ears of yours this time." She opened her purse, put her gloves inside, dug around, and took out her lipstick. She walked over to the lavatory mirror, carefully applied lipstick to her mouth, dabbed some on her fingertip and smeared red on her cheeks. She clicked her purse shut and wheeled around.

"A week ago, you and your mother were in a car crash outside of Hickory Creek. The police contacted me because I'm next of kin... your mother is my daughter." She returned to Freddy's bedside. "And so that makes you my grandson," she said, pinching him on the cheek.

"Ouch!" Freddy flinched and jerked away. Memory of his hospital stay rushed back. He struggled to sit up. Bits and pieces of a crash flashed through his mind. "I want to see my mother."

Freddy's grandmother shook her head. "Not at this time." She bent over and whispered in his ear. "Your mother is in a coma. You're coming with me now."

Freddy had no idea what she was talking about, and twisted the edge of the sheet, panic rising in his chest. "Where's my mother?!"

Mrs. Webbe tapped the bed railing and made a clucking sound with her tongue. "Bruster County Hospital." She strolled to the window and blinked against the glare.

"Where's that?" Freddy said.

"About twenty-five miles from here."

Freddy stared, dumbfounded, thinking, *"I don't want to go with this woman. What's gonna happen to me?"*

Freddy uttered under his breath, "Mama."

"So Francis," Mrs. Webbe said, "for now you're going to come with me. This really is quite an opportunity. You'll be attending Wiggins Preparatory in the fall with all of the boys and girls who *rate* in St. Wigbod."

Freddy didn't care. All he wanted was his life back with his mom at Hickory Creek, but it was already fading into a dim memory.

Parked at the loading area of the hospital was a black limousine. The driver, a young man, mid- twenties, dressed in black livery, shot out of the car, opened the passenger rear door, and stood at attention. Freddy noticed his crooked smile and chipped front tooth. His cap

14

squeezed down a mass of black curly hair. To Freddy's astonishment, Grandmother Webbe got in, and gestured for him to follow.

Freddy settled into the roomy backseat. "Are we going to visit Mama?"

Mrs. Webb sat up stiffly. "No, we are not." She gave him a harsh look. "You're testing the limits of my patience," she said, her voice rising.

Freddy was shocked. "I don't even know you. You say you're my grandmother but you're acting mean."

*I don't want to go with her. I want to see my mother.*

Freddy tried the car door handle but it was locked. He cried out, "Where are you taking me?"

"I knew this wasn't going to work," Mrs. Webbe said. "You need to calm down, young man." She said to the driver, "Charles, get us home as soon as possible."

Freddy felt prickles of hate for this woman. "Why won't you let me know about my mother?" he stammered. He could feel his eyes welling up. "Why can't I see her?" He wiped his runny nose on his shirt sleeve.

Mrs. Webbe dug in her purse and tossed a tissue to Freddy. "I was trying to save you from the gory details but you won't cooperate...I'm sorry to have to tell you this. Your mother is clinging to life. The doctors at the County

Hospital have her in an induced coma. You can't see her right now because she is in the Advanced Life Support Unit."

A vision of his mother hugging him flashed through his mind. "Will she be alright?"

"They're doing the best they can."

A huge, weighty sadness swept over him. *Somehow I'm going to get away from this witch.*

"Charles, in case you haven't figured it out by now," Mrs. Webbe said, as her chauffeur put the engine into gear and pulled into traffic, "this is my grandson, Francis. I apologize that you had to be a party to this ugly conversation."

"My name isn't Francis. It's Freddy," he said.

"Don't *be common.* No nicknames. You were named after your great, great, great grandfather, Sir Francis Snarsbrough, one of the original settlers of Jamestowne," Mrs. Webbe boasted and her voice became shrill. "You come from a long line of aristocratic ancestors, Francis. You must live up to your legacy." She adjusted the air conditioner vent and the bird on her hat jiggled.

From her attaché, she took out a notebook and reviewed what was written there. She looked over at Freddy, her eyes narrowing. "You will be attending Wiggins Preparatory in September. First on the agenda—a

.

haircut." She tugged on his blonde, rooster- tailed cowlick. "You need one."

Freddy jerked his head to the side and stared out the window, his vision blurry. The droning of her voice made his head pound, and he tried to focus on the passing scenery.

Freddy's palms were dripping with sweat. He wiped them on his new khaki pants, leaving a wet streak. Mrs. Webbe glanced at Freddy, "Now look what you've done!" She rubbed her forehead. "I'm getting a headache."

The car traveled about three miles before turning onto a lane flanked by giant poplar trees. The limousine slowed and stopped before an enormous wrought iron gate; Freddy looked up to read the words across the entrance to Grandmother Webbe's estate: *Eagles' Nest*. Charles punched in the code on a metal box, and the gate swung open to a magnificent garden of flowers and shrubs. Freddy could not believe how vast the grounds were.

Then he saw the house.

The Bavarian mansion was perched on the highest point in St. Wigbod. Three huge chimneys rose up from the high-pitched gables of the red-brick, three-story Tudor. A bay window supported by decorative corbels graced the second floor of the house. The crisscrossing half-timbered wood on the second story made Freddy think of the house from Hansel and Gretel.

The limousine rolled to a stop at the side entrance under the portico. Access to this part of the house, he would learn, was reserved for close family members and employees. Freddy reached for the door handle. Grandmother Webbe clucked her tongue in disapproval and nodded at Charles who was making his way to the side of the car. "Patience…please."

The door opened and Charles stepped back, allowing Freddy to get out. The chauffeur then offered Mrs. Webbe his hand.

Mrs. Webbe led the way up the outside steps to the side doorway. Freddy stopped to corral a lady bug from a bush. "Come along," she said, "don't dawdle," Freddy let the ladybug go. She shook her head. *Just like your father—man~a~na , man~a~na.*

A plump, short, middle-aged woman appeared at the door, her white, wiry hair poking out from under a black mesh hairnet. Her black uniform was covered by a starched white pinafore apron. "Welcome! Welcome!" she gushed.

"Francis, this is Mrs. McVicker, our housekeeper," Mrs. Webbe said. "I expect you to treat her with courtesy and respect."

Mrs. McVicker made a small curtsy, beaming with joy. "Please, allow me to show you to your room, sir."

Mrs. Webbe bent down to meet Freddy at eye level. "Your bedroom is on the second floor in the west wing. You are to stay in that area," she said. "I don't want to hear you've been roaming all over or snooping about. Are we clear about this?"

"Yes, Mrs. Webbe," Freddy said. He craned his neck trying to take in the vastness of the house.

"*Mrs. Webbe?*" Charles said entering the house. "Why, son, this is your grandma!"

Shaking her head, Mrs. Webbe said, "Absolutely not, Charles. I don't want to be called *Grandma!*"

Charles looked surprised.

"Although I will allow Grandmother," she added. "You may address me as Grandmother Webbe."

Freddy nodded. *Why is she so cold and distant? Somehow, I am going to escape this place and get back home to Hickory Creek and Mama.*

Mrs. Webbe added, "Mrs. McVicker will be seeing to your needs and your meals." Freddy could hear the disdain in her voice.

She sighed and looked at her watch. "Is there anything else before I leave you with Mrs. McVicker?"

Freddy shifted from one foot to the other. "When will I be able to see Mama?"

Mrs. Webbe exhaled her exasperation. "I thought I had made myself clear, Francis. I don't know why you can't understand this—your mother is very ill. You would only make her condition worse by visiting her before she is ready. Is that what you want?"

Freddy shook his head. A burst of loneliness filled his heart.

"FINALLY!" She turned, threw up her hands, and entered the house.

Mrs. McVicker looked at Freddy with a befuddled expression and shrugged in apology; then a smile spread over her face. "Come along, Francis. Let's see your room, shall we?"

Mrs. McVicker led Freddy from the back entry-way through the mud room, down a hallway and up the narrow, steep servant's stairs. On the second floor, Mrs. McVicker hurried down another hall and then stopped in front of a white door in need of a fresh coat of paint. The key was hard to turn but Mrs. McVicker jiggled it until the door unlocked. Freddy peered in at the musty smelling room. On the windows hung heavy, red velvet drapes. At one end of the room was a double bed with an oversized headboard engraved with cherubs. Matching marble-topped tables flanked each side of the bed. In one corner a knick-knack shelf was home to a variety of angel statuettes. In the other corner was some kind of shrine. Candles of different colors and shapes sat atop a table adorned with white lace. Figurines in colorful robes holding spears stood guard. A worn Persian carpet covered the discolored hardwood floor. For some strange reason Freddy felt a familiar presence. Flashes of his mother on the bed, crying, flickered through his mind.

"This will be your room," Mrs. McVicker said. "It hasn't been used in quite a while. Mrs. Webbe used to come up here, but that's been years now." Mrs. McVicker walked across the room, pulled back the drapes and opened the windows. A whoosh of dust blew in. "We hadn't the time to do much more than clean your bathroom and change the sheets, but Mister Charles and me will give your room a complete makeover this weekend."

Freddy took a deep breath and the two stood quietly for a moment, searching for something to say.

"Your bathroom is through that door," Mrs. McVicker said pointing to the door directly across from the bed. She opened it to reveal a full-length mirror.

Mrs. McVicker looked down at her hands and twisted her ring. "Also, Mrs. Webbe would prefer for you to use the servant's stairs. She just thought that it would

.

make more sense and you can come and go more freely that way."

Freddy gazed across the room. A yellow Formica and chrome table leaning against the window captured his attention. Beside it was a chrome chair of worn yellow vinyl, matching tape covering its many rips and tears.

"I know it doesn't look like a boy's room right now, Francis, but Mister Charles and me will find some things to make this room homier. In the meantime, try to adjust." Almost as an afterthought she said, "I've got some fresh baked oatmeal cookies down in the kitchen." She hurried to the door, trilling, "Cookies and milk, cookies and milk – they'll make you stand tall in your kilt."

"That's OK," Freddy smiled weakly. "I'm not hungry." He went over to the bed and flopped down. His mattress was as hard as a rock. Freddy screamed at the top of his lungs, "I want to go home!"

# CHAPTER 4
# A FRIGHTFUL NIGHT

That evening, Mrs. McVicker brought Freddy a radio, a grilled cheese sandwich, a glass of milk, and warm oatmeal cookies. He sat on his bed devouring the sandwich and listening to K-ROD, the rock 'n' roll station, until he drifted off to sleep.

Jolted awake by a flutter on the bed, Freddy heard crunching and rattling. Something moved across his hand! He jumped up and reached for the bedside lamp. Light filled the room to reveal huge black cockroaches scattering throughout the room, many disappearing under the baseboards. Freddy grabbed his shoe and took aim at the monstrous insects, banging and crushing them on the floor. One dazed roach flew at Freddy, its sticky legs grabbing the opening to Freddy's shirt, disappearing inside. Freddy screamed, ripped the buttons from his new shirt, and tore it off. The roach fell to the floor and vanished.

He scanned the room, his heart racing, but the bugs had retreated. He pulled off his other shoe, and slipped under the covers, tucking the sheets close to his body, gripping a shoe in each hand. Freddy did not dare turn the light off. He spent the rest of the night huddled against the headboard, his mind aware of every creak. At some point, he fell asleep.

Freddy awoke the next morning, his head pounding, shoulders stiff and aching. He closed his eyes as he stretched and bent over, touching the floor, and felt the hard shell and gooey remains of one of the roaches in last night's attack. His hand recoiled as he remembered the nightmare. He leapt back onto the bed and eyed the room for live roaches. Finally, he decided he was safe, at least, for the moment.

He hurried to put on his khaki pants, t-shirt and tennis shoes, then high-stepped out of the room to avoid the gooey corpses. As Freddy neared the kitchen, he heard Mrs. McVicker singing.

Freddy stood in the doorway until Mrs. McVicker looked up. "Good morning, Francis! Come in and have yourself a seat. I'm making pancakes."

Freddy glanced around the room, looking for any sign of vermin—an antenna, hairy legs, beady eyes—anything that might indicate their hiding places. Hesitantly he took a seat.

"Smells good," Freddy said, although his stomach felt queasy.

Mrs. McVicker smiled, revealing her stubby teeth, and put a plate of pancakes at his place. "Did you sleep well?"

Freddy looked at the plate and his stomach curdled. "No! No, I didn't!"

Concern spread across Mrs. McVicker's face.

"It was the worst night of my life!" Freddy said, his voice rising. "My room is infested with cockroaches…they were crawling on me, on the bed until I turned on the light."

"How frightful!" Mrs. McVicker shuddered, and wrung her hands.

"There must have been a thousand of them!" he said, stabbing a pancake. He took a bite and spit it out. Freddy covered his mouth… "I'm gonna be sick!" He began to heave but made it to the bathroom in time.

Mrs. McVicker threw up her hands. "Horrors! We haven't used that wing of the house since his mother——," her voice trailed off.

When Freddy staggered back to the kitchen, Mrs. McVicker handed him a washcloth. "Wipe your face and you'll feel better."

Freddy's stomach did a flip-flop.

She patted his back, assuring him Charles would take care of the problem.

"I hope so!" Freddy said. "I won't stay in that creepy bug-infested room another night. This place is like a house of horrors, only worse!"

Mrs. McVicker poured a small glass of orange juice, put the juice bottle in the refrigerator and turned to Freddy. "Don't worry, dear. It will be spick and span by this evening. Oh, before I forget…your grandmother's waiting for you in her study. She would be beside herself if she knew about your nasty visitors. Let's keep this to ourselves, shall we?"

Freddy nodded and pushed away the plate of pancakes. "I don't want these."

"You need to keep your strength up."

"I said I don't want any," his voice rose. "I wish everyone would just leave me alone."

Mrs. McVicker looked hurt. "Well, if that's the way you want it, I'll try not to interfere, Mr. Griswold."

Freddy looked down at the table. "I'm sorry. It's not your fault. I just want to see my mother."

"Here, drink your orange juice. You'll feel better. And don't you worry. Charles and me are on your side."

He shrugged and sipped some juice. Then he followed Mrs. McVicker through the butler's pantry, past the dining room, the library, the formal parlor, and into the study.

Dressed in a grey suit, her red hair in a bun, Grandmother Webbe was on the phone and motioned for Freddy to sit in a high-back leather chair. When her conversation was over, she looked at Freddy as though she was examining him under a microscope. She sighed and shook her head. "I don't know what to do about you. I was on the phone with your former public school, P.S. something or another. It seems your grades were less than stellar, although, you did manage a B in physical education. You're not going to get anywhere in life unless you buckle down."

Mrs. Webbe rose from her chair, walked to the fireplace and checked the mantle for dust. "I'm going to have to pull some strings to get you into Wiggins. They only want the best and brightest."

Freddy's head was splitting with pain. He took a deep breath, as his mom had taught him to do whenever he got bad headaches. *I've got to get out of here.*

Mrs. Webbe picked up a book on her desk and leafed through the pages, shaking her head. "I don't know if you can make it at Wiggins." She lifted her eyes from the page. "You look like a ragamuffin in those dirty pants. All I can do is try to make something out of you, Francis. Heaven only knows your mother hasn't."

*Witch!* The pounding in Freddy's head became worse. Pressure was building in his chest. "Don't talk about my mother like that," he said. Freddy approached his grandmother, arms stiff, eyes bulging. "I want to see my mother!"

"Don't use that tone with me, young man," she shot back.

Freddy choked back his tears but stood his ground. "I want to see my mother," he said again.

"Now I think we're all under a strain," Mrs. Webbe said. "So many adjustments. I'm going to send you to see …uh…a doctor... Dr. Pickhouse. He might be able to help you." Mrs. Webbe narrowed her eyes, returned to her writing desk, and scribbled on note paper. "I'll make an appointment for you."

She looked up at Freddy, pursed her lips, and waved her hand in dismissal. "That's all." *I don't know if I can stand having him here.*

Freddy, trembling with rage, fled the room. Somehow, he found his way back through the maze of rooms to the door that led to the abandoned second floor. Abandoned. Just like him. He opened the door to his room and stopped dead in his tracks when he remembered his roommates. The scattered roach remains were still on the floor. Standing in the middle of the room, Freddy screamed, over and over, "Mama, come get me!"

Exhausted, he plopped on the bed. Anguish and rage penetrated his whole being. Freddy pounded his bed until his knuckles were swollen. Then he curled up, wrapped his arms around his body, and moaned. Finally, he rolled over on his side and fell asleep. It was not a deep sleep, rather a light doze filled with dreams. He thought of his best friend, Jeremy, and roaming the woods together, setting up bottles for target practice. He thought of living with Jeremy. His heart ached. He wanted his mother.

When he woke, it was well into the afternoon. Groggy and disoriented, he gazed about his room. An assortment of books had been stacked neatly on the Formica table. He rolled off the bed and noticed his floor had been swept clean. The curtains were tied back, the afternoon sun flowing in. On his bed was a folded note. Freddy opened it and smiled when he read—"Don't be late for supper...we're having French fried cockroaches. — Charles."

He sighed, shaking his head, and made his way to the table to review the books.

None of them looked interesting, but he picked up *Pocahontas and Captain John Smith* and skimmed the first page…snakes, alligators, mosquitoes, death, Indians. He flipped through the pages, occasionally stopping to look at an illustration before tossing the book back on the table.

There was a knock at the door. "Time for dinner, Francis," Mrs. McVicker peeked her head into the room and surveyed the floor. "Wash your hands and come down."

Freddy didn't answer. *I hope the witch isn't eating with us.*

With clean hands and combed hair, Freddy opened his bedroom door to the sumptuous aroma of Mrs. McVicker's cooking. He made his way down the back stairs, feeling like a stepchild being hidden away.

The kitchen had a warm, cozy feel; a pot was simmering on the stove. The round oak table was set for three; a vase of pink roses decorated the center. Freddy was glad to see his favorite food being served— macaroni and cheese.

Charles sauntered into the kitchen, leaned around Mrs. McVicker, grabbed a green bean from the pot, and popped it into his mouth, "OooWee, that's good! Come on, let's eat."

Each pulled out a chair, and covered their laps with a napkin. Freddy took a heaping serving of macaroni and cheese, preparing to gulp it down when he noticed Mrs.

McVicker's outstretched arms on the table, palms up. Charles placed his palm in hers, reached over and took hold of Freddy's hand. "Let's bless this food." he said.

Freddy's face burned with embarrassment.

Charles gave a short blessing, and then asked, "So, Francis, what did you do today?"

"Nothing," Freddy said, chewing on a chicken leg.

"Now, I know you did something to pass all that time upstairs."

"What I did was try to figure out a way to get out of this place and see my mother."

"I left you some books," Mrs. McVicker said. "Did you look at any of those?"

"Yeah, I flipped through one," Freddy said, reaching for another drumstick.

Charles took a bite of macaroni and cheese. "What was it about?"

"I don't know, Charles. I said I was just flipping through the pages."

"Someone's been eating mean beans," Charles said.

Freddy stared at his plate and said nothing.

"You know, Francis," Charles said, "we've been bending over backwards to make you feel as comfortable as possible. So if you want to have a pity party, go on, but it's not going to solve anything."

Silence followed.

Charles said, "When I was real young, my mom died. You're lucky. You still have yours."

"I'm sorry," he said. "I'm just so miserable."

"I know you miss your mom," Charles said, "but in the meantime, it might help to do something you like."

"Yeah, I guess so... Uh, Charles, I was wondering...do you have any books about cars?"

"Are you kiddin'? I've got a big stash. Mostly *Hot Rod*. You interested in cars?"

"Kind of," Freddy said in a monotone. "Don't know anything about them, though."

"Tell you what." Charles leaned his chair back on two legs. "I've got this old car I'm fixin' up. A 'rat rod'. Maybe I could bring it over and we could work on it."

"Yeah. Maybe. Sure," Freddy said his voice growing distant. "If my grandmother lets me."

"If it was presented right," Charles said, "she just might. People can surprise you."

"Sounds like fun." He was trying to sound excited but his mind was drifting to thoughts of his mother. *I've got to see her.*

## CHAPTER 5
## THE QUELL STONE

The next morning Charles dropped Freddy off at the front entrance to Webbe Memorial.

"I'll be back to pick you up in one hour. Right here. Don't get lost." Charles waved as he pulled away.

The enormous lobby of the hospital reminded Freddy of a fancy hotel; a multi-tiered chandelier hung above elegant tapestry chairs. Freddy wandered around by himself looking for Suite 721 SW until he finally asked a volunteer for directions.

"Take the elevator to the seventh floor," the man said. "Turn right, proceed to the nurse's station, and bear left to the end of the hall. You can't miss it."

Freddy peeked inside the office of Dr. Pickhouse. Soft elevator music played in the reception area. The scent of lilac filled the air.

"May, I help you?" a woman said, her voice soft.

Freddy pulled at the hem of his polo shirt; his hands dripping with sweat. "Uh, I think I've got an appointment."

"Are you Francis Griswold?"

"Yes 'um." Freddy noticed her name tag. — Jewel. She sat erect. Sparkling stones adorned the black frames of her egg-shaped glasses. Her auburn hair was pinned in a French twist with a pencil stuck in the side.

Jewel pointed to an office. She said, "Dr. Pickhouse is expecting you. Go right on in."

Freddy stood in the office door, the smell of pipe tobacco wafting in the air. A wreath of smoke encircled Dr. Pickhouse's head. He was chewing on a black pipe, engrossed in writing. He reminded Freddy of Santa Claus with his long white beard and mustache. His office was cluttered with wadded-up papers and unshelved books. Discarded French fry containers trashed the floor and the wastepaper basket overflowed; bits of pipe tobacco littered his desk and the Oriental carpet.

Dr. Pickhouse, scribbling on a yellow note pad became aware of the presence at his door.

The jolly looking doctor scooted his chair back, got up, stumbled on a book and knocked the wastepaper basket over. Out spilled crumpled paper, pencil shavings and apple cores. "Jewel," he called. "Bring the broom and dust pan."

Freddy looked from the waiting room to the office. His face felt hot, his palms clammy. Dr. Pickhouse extended his right hand, then grabbed Freddy pulling him in for a bear hug. Freddy's eyes bulged; he gasped for air while the doctor held him tight. *Do all doctors welcome patients like this?*

"Come on in and have a seat," the doctor said, a big smile spreading across his face. "The last time I saw you, you were just a baby and sitting on your mama's lap."

Jewel hurried in, cleaned up the mess and left. Freddy inhaled deeply, brushed pipe tobacco off the seat of the chair and steadied himself on the edge.

Dr. Pickhouse studied Freddy's demeanor and pulled his desk chair up close. He searched for a clean yellow tablet, sharpened his pencil and sighed. "Your grandmother called me. She's worried about you."

Freddy rolled his eyes; his hands clinched together.

"What do you think her concerns might be, Francis?"

"My name is Freddy...Freddy." The veins on his neck distended followed by throbbing in his ears.

"Okay. Then Freddy it is."

"What kind of doctor are you anyway?" Are you going to experiment on my brain or something?" Freddy said.

"No, no, no. I just want to help you with your feelings," Dr. Pickhouse said, scribbling on his yellow pad. He leaned back in his chair and waited for Freddy to speak.

A knot growing in Freddy's throat prevented him from uttering a sound. Jumbled thoughts filled his mind, *My life has changed so quickly. It's cruel and unjust. Why me? We had a perfect life.*

Dr. Pickhouse reached across his desk and grabbed two CarPops from a jar, "I'm here to help if I can." He handed Freddy the Pops, then reached in for another. "Put one in your pocket for later" They unwrapped and admired the make and model of their sweet treats.

Dr. Pickhouse said, "Tell me about anything that's bothering you. What we discuss in here is just between you and me." He gazed into Freddy's eyes. "Believe me?"

"I guess." Freddy looked at his trembling hands and fidgeted in his seat. "Okay," …. he hesitated. Looking at the floor, speaking softly, Freddy said, "My mom's in the hospital and I haven't seen her. My grandmother won't let me." His eyes welled up and he gazed at the framed Rorschach images behind the doctor. He put his head in his hands. When he finally looked up at Dr Pickhouse, he felt calmer. *I don't care what she says, I'm going to see Mom no matter what it takes.*

Dr. Pickhouse stopped writing and the two sat in silence. Then the doctor scratched his head and cleared his throat. "Freddy, what do you remember about the accident?"

Freddy closed his eyes and rubbed his forehead. "I remember it was raining...hard. We were coming up on Highland Tunnel. I rolled down the window and stuck my head out trying to see the lines on the edge of the road. I saw a bright light coming at us as we entered the tunnel. Mom swerved right...that's all I remember."

The doctor patted Freddy on the shoulder. "That's a lot to think about," he said. "You're lucky to be alive." He rummaged through his desk drawer. "You say you haven't seen your mom?"

Freddy furrowed his brow and nodded.

"Well that's the first matter of business to sort out. I'll talk to your grandmother. Ah, here it is."

He placed in Freddy's hand, a black, smooth stone, the size of a pullet egg. "This is a Quell Stone," Dr. Pickhouse said. "It eases worry. Carry it with you wherever you go, and rub it when you feel sad or lonely or afraid."

Freddy stared at the stone. He suddenly felt calm and thought it was the shiniest rock he had ever seen.

"Ponder what is true, what is noble," Dr. Pickhouse said, "and what is right. Rub this stone and your fear, and sadness, and loneliness will dissipate. When the stone turns white, tiny silver and gold sparks will shoot out and you will be guarded and protected."

"Thank you." Freddy rubbed the stone as he slipped it into his pants' pocket. His pocket came alive as the stone spit sparks out the seams. "Oh, that's weird. It kind of tickles. I can hardly wait to show Charles."

Dr. Pickhouse laughed and broke wind at the same time. Freddy exploded with laughter. By the time the Quell Stone had worked its magic, Freddy was feeling less worried. "I'll be sure to thank Grandmother Webbe for sending me to a psychiatrist."

"When it comes to your grandmother, I suggest that you stick to the word *doctor*."

On the elevator ride to the lobby, Freddy pulled out the stone and rubbed it. An image of his mother jostling his hair jolted him. *"Freddy, darling! I want to see you."* As quickly as she appeared, his mother's image faded. "Mama?" His voice echoed in the elevator. He gazed at the stone and wondered if he could use it to make his grandmother disappear.

# CHAPTER 6
# HITCHHIKING

Outside the hospital, Freddy glanced around for Charles. *What's taking him so long?* Freddy reached into his pants' pocket and gently rubbed the Quell Stone and felt it rumble. Something resembling static electricity stung him. He yanked his hand back and stared at his fingers.

He reflected on his meeting. He liked Dr. Pickhouse and felt he had found a confidante…maybe he could trust Dr. Pickhouse. Freddy's smile faded, as he thought of the accident and his mother. He was desperate to see her. Then, he remembered what the doctor had said. "That's the first matter of business to sort out."

Freddy noticed a bus stopping at the end of the hospital driveway and an unexpected idea hit him. He hurried back to the information desk.

A gray-haired elderly lady in a pink and white striped apron smiled at Freddy. He cleared his throat. "Excuse me. Do you know what bus I would take to Bruster County Hospital?"

"Oh my goodness, that's a long way." She stood to study the area map behind her desk. "It's on Bruster Road, which would be the number 12."

Freddy moved to a nearby window, squinted at the bus, spotted a number 12 above the windshield and shot out the door.

"It looks like it's about twenty miles out," she said. "I don't know if the buses go that far." She turned.

Freddy was gone.

Freddy ran at the bus, arms waving, as it pulled past the hospital and spit exhaust at the stop. He glanced around for any sign of Charles, then stuck his thumb up. At least a dozen cars and trucks whizzed by. A big 18-wheeler pulled to the side of the road, showering the pavement with gravel. The driver leaned out the window. "Want a ride, kid?" He had a hacking cough and spit tobacco juice out the window.

Freddy hesitated, but the prospect of seeing his mother overcame him. He approached the passenger side of the rig and had to stand on his tip-toes to reach the door handle. When he got the door open and saw the condition of the cab, he was appalled. Beer bottles were strewn about, fast food wrappers littered the floor, and the smell of whisky was overwhelming.

The driver said, "I'd been needin' some company. Hop on up and let's have a beer."

Freddy jumped back and closed the door. "Thanks anyway. I see my ride coming." Freddy's heart was racing. *That was a close call. No telling where I might have ended up. I hope somebody besides a creepy drunk stops."*

About five minutes later, an old truck slowed down and rolled to a stop, its breaks screeching. Freddy wasn't certain if the driver was stopping for him or if the sputtering engine had simply given out where he was. Freddy's legs felt frozen in place.

A wizened, weathered face peered out the window. "Where you goin'?"

Freddy regained control of his legs and slowly approached the driver. He cleared his throat, "I need to get to Bruster County Hospital. Are you going that way?"

"Yeah, am. Git in."

\*\*\*\*\*\*

Traffic came to a standstill. Grimacing, Charles hit the steering wheel. The road was blocked off. Charles rolled down the window and called out to a policeman, "What's the holdup?"

"Farmer lost a load of hay."

"How long before it's cleaned up?"

41

"Shouldn't be too long....maybe twenty minutes."

Charles checked his watch. He wouldn't be too late, maybe five minutes or so. His hands gripped the steering wheel and he felt his heart pounding. He honked his horn, and the car behind him honked and then another, until a cacophony of horns filled the air.

Slowly his lane began to move. Charles passed a line of cars on the right shoulder, picked up speed, swerved back into his lane and flew through a yellow light.

At the patient pick-up, Charles screeched to a stop as the sputtering truck limped into traffic, coughing a black cloud of smoke in its trail. Charles set the engine in park, opened the latest issue of *Hot Rod* and thumbed the pages. He checked his watch. — still no sign of Freddy. He tossed the magazine in the back seat.

Charles entered the lobby and spotted the information desk. "Have you seen a boy— blonde hair— rooster tail?" Charles tried to sound calm.

"Why yes, I did… looking for a ride out to Bruster County on the bus," the clerk replied.

Charles' mind was racing. *Maybe he's running away.*

Charles' legs felt weak, "Oh my gosh!  Which way did he go?"

The desk clerk said, "I ran out to let him know that buses don't go out that far.  I saw him talking to a guy in a big rig.  I watched him for a while and then he got into an old pickup."

She pointed to the intersection where a thin veil of exhaust still hung in the air.  "I don't think they could've gotten far," she added as Charles sprinted out the door.

His instincts told him Freddy was on his way to see his mother.  *Mrs. Webbe shouldn't be so hard-headed all the time. Shouldn't keep a boy from his mother.*

Charles turned onto Bruster Road.  A nauseating trail of fumes filled the air.  His mind was full of wild thoughts. *What if he's kidnapped?* Charles scrutinized the road ahead as the air grew thicker and blacker. The limo slowed down to go around an old junk truck stalled halfway off the road.  A stooped black man was peering through steam rising from under the hood.  Freddy was retrieving a bucket of water from the bed.

Charles let out a sigh, the tightness in his stomach relaxing.  He pulled the limo onto the shoulder and casually got out.  "Need any help?"

43

"Sho do," the old man said.

Freddy dropped the bucket, sloshing water onto the road, and ran up to Charles stammering. "The doctor let me out early so I decided to hitch a ride."

"Uh, huh. So where were you hitching a ride to?"

"Charles, let me introduce you to a very interesting man," Freddy said.

The old man turned, wiped dirt onto a red rag and extended his calloused hand. "Name's Boangeres...call me Bo." His bib overalls were worn and spotted with grease and paint.

Charles clasped his hands behind his neck and spun around. "What were you thinking? Were you just going to let me wait there all afternoon? Your grandmother...Oh, I was scared out of my wits."

"I'm sorry Charles."

"Now don't be too hard on da boy. He's a fine one. Bin tellin' me 'bout his mother in da hospital." Bo was a loud, animated talker. "The Lord was with 'em. Alleluia!" Bo said, raising his arms skyward.

Charles took a deep breath and helped Freddy fetch the water. Charles then instructed Freddy on how the radiator uses water to keep the engine cool, and Bo told them of his life as a sharecropper and lay minister for the

Colored Baptist Church in South St. Wigbod. He invited them to visit on Sunday for a 'real spiritual revival.'

"I sure appreciate the invitation," Charles said. "Well, it looks like you're all fixed up." Shaking Bo's hand, he continued, "Thanks for taking care of our boy."

"I'z glad for the company. Take care, now."

The drive back to town was filled with silence. Freddy stared out the front side window, blowing air vapor onto the glass. He reached into his pocket and fingered the stone. "Want a CarPop?" Freddy said quietly.

"I'm at a loss, "Charles said. "I should tell your grandmother."

"Don't—please. I promise I won't pull something stupid like that again." Freddy glanced from Charles to his hands and sighed. He was already thinking of ways to get to the hospital. "I just wanted to see my mother." Freddy whispered.

Charles pulled into a parking lot, rolled down the windows and turned off the engine.

"I'm going to tell you something. It might help you get a handle on things." Charles took a deep breath, and faced Freddy. "Even if you had made it to County you wouldn't have been able to see your mom. The doctors put her in a coma to keep her brain from swelling. She's in the Critical Care Unit."

Freddy bit his lip and covered his face with his hands. Rivers of tears streamed down his cheeks. Finally, he managed to catch his breath. "Is she going to get well?"

Charles said, "From what I hear she has a fifty-fifty chance."

# CHAPTER 7
# WHO'S MIGUEL?

It was a warm sunny day when Freddy had the idea to go exploring. He decided this would be a good time to investigate his new home and slip into the garden. However, nothing helped tame his worry and heartache for his mother.

Mrs. Webbe was at a Jamestowne Society Convention in Washington D.C. and wouldn't return until Sunday evening, the day before school started. During the day he was left to himself while Charles and Mrs. McVicker were preoccupied with their responsibilities.

Freddy wandered downstairs. The sting of learning about his mother's condition was still raw. Freddy headed to his grandmother's study and peeked in. He looked over his shoulder. A feeling of animosity filled his stomach. *Her desk. Her precious desk... Control Central.*

Freddy gazed at the desk and then entered the room and stealthfully pulled opened the drawer. *Everything's so neat and precise. She makes me sick.*

On top of the well organized drawer was a leather bound address book. *Maybe the number of the hospital's in here.*

Freddy thumbed through the book; a picture was jammed into the center section. He pulled it out. It was a photo of his mother holding a baby and a young guy with his arm around her shoulder. He turned the black and white photo over. 'Hannah, Francis and Miguel— 1944' were written on the back. Freddy quickly stuck the photo back into place. "Who's Miguel?" he said.

Freddy turned to the B section. There it was. Bruster County Hospital… Next to the phone number in precise printing were the words Bruster County —BR2365.

Freddy picked up the phone and dialed. An operator answered, "Bruster County Hospital."

Freddy's heart pounded. "Hannah Griswold." He sounded like he had a mouth full of cotton.

"I'm sorry, sir but she's in Advanced Life Support."

"Hey, Freddy," Charles said as he entered the room, sauntering over to the desk. "I've been looking for you."

Freddy quickly hung up the phone.

Charles looked at the open desk drawer and the address book. "What're you doing? Were you calling your mama?"

Freddy said, "Yes, I was." His voice rising. "I want to see my mother."

Charles pulled up a chair next to the desk. "Oh boy! Okay! I hear you." He reached for a tissue and handed it to Freddy. They sat in silence. Freddy wiped his nose on his sleeve.

"Charles, I need your help. If you hear anything about Mom, you have to let me know."

Charles patted Freddy's leg, "I will, Freddy. I promise."

After that, Freddy was careful not to venture beyond his bedroom in the cavernous west wing. He spent hours reading Charles' *Hot Rod* magazines, learning about various car parts, and custom additions.

In the evening, he'd have dinner with Charles and Mrs. McVicker. While she washed the dishes, Charles and Freddy pieced together a model of a '57 Chevrolet Charles had brought home as a surprise. Freddy introduced Charles to his favorite rock 'n' roll station, K-ROD... one night he even imitated dancers on the Steve Bosno dance show, *The Hop*.

Every night, before he went to bed, he wrote to his mother about his day, and how much he wanted to see her. In the last letter he wrote, he asked, "Who's Miguel?"

The night before he was to start school at Wiggins Preparatory, Freddy lay on his bed worried about his first day. Charles had gone to pick up Mrs. Webbe at the airport. Mrs. McVicker invited Freddy to watch *The Ed Sullivan Show* and see the mouse puppet, Topo Gigio, but he was too nervous to settle in front of the TV.

Up in his room, Freddy worried about his classmates at the new school. *Would they be friendly or stuck-up?* Freddy's stomach churned and he yearned for his mother's reassurance. He couldn't stand the thought of her alone at the hospital surrounded by cold machines.

Freddy noticed that Mrs. McVicker had hung his freshly pressed school uniform on the hook of his closet door. His new attire included a tie—a challenge Charles had been helping him with— , a crisp forest green oxford shirt with the school insignia on the pocket, khaki pants, a brown belt, forest green socks, and his Weejuns— brown penny loafers.

His stomach tightened again. He put his head down on his arms crossing his knees. Then, he began to think of all the people who were trying to help him. *Charles had said, "If you want to have a pity-party, then do it, but it's not going to change anything."*

*Maybe Charles was right. All I have been doing is thinking about myself. Mrs. McVicker's food is awesome. Charles chauffeurs me around and spends time with me working on models and even Grandmother Webbe has given me a place to stay.* Freddy felt different in a way he could not explain. He could cry and stomp his feet but in the end nothing changed. If he wanted to survive this ordeal, maybe he was going to have to do some changing.

Finally, Freddy kicked off his shoes, pulled off his clothes, peeled back his bed sheets, and slid in between the covers. Still cautious about six-legged intruders, he kept the light on and reached for his class schedule on the night table. He reviewed each line again, imagining a face to match each teacher's name. Before long, he drifted off to sleep.

| WIGGINS PREPARATORY CLASS SCHEDULE | | | |
|---------|----------|-------------|-------------|
| Class | Teacher | Time | Room |
| History | Gore | 9:00-9:55 | 101 |
| Math | Profit | 10:00-10:55 | 124 |
| Music | Flowers | 11:00-11:55 | Music |
| Lunch | XXX | 12:00-12:25 | Cafeteria |
| Science | Studley | 12:30-1:25 | 200 |
| P.E. | Beast | 1:30-2:25 | Field House |
| English | Scales | 2:30-3:30 | 100 |
| Student: Freddy Griswold | | | |

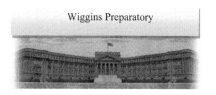

# CHAPTER 8
## FIRST DAY AT THE GRAND LADY

Freddy woke to loud knocking on his door.

"Rise and shine," Charles hollered, opening the door. Freddy buried his face in his pillow.

"Come on. Get up," Charles said, pulling the covers off the bed.

Freddy grabbed an edge of sheet. "Charles, stop it. That's not funny!"

"It won't be funny if your ride leaves without you. You've got fifteen minutes to get dressed and get downstairs for breakfast. The limo is leaving in thirty."

By the time Freddy reached the kitchen, he was too nervous to eat. Mrs. McVicker beamed seeing Freddy in his uniform. She had cooked up a feast of fried eggs, skillet fries, sausages, wheat toast, and orange juice. He nibbled on a piece of toast, and gulped some orange juice before racing to the bathroom gagging.

At half past seven, Charles pulled the limo under the portico and entered the kitchen for a cup of coffee. As

Freddy returned from the bathroom, Charles let out a whistle. "If I didn't know better I'd think we had a bona fide Wiggie right here in our kitchen. My, my, you sure do look preppy."

Mrs. McVicker nodded and filled Charles' cup with coffee.

Mrs. McVicker giggled and said, "Your grandmother wants to inspect— I mean see you before you go to school."

"Mrs. McVicker... Charles," Freddy said, his voice cracking, "I just want to say that if it weren't for you two I...I...just...don't..."

Mrs. McVicker padded over to Freddy, put her arms around him and patted him on the shoulder. "There, there, Francis Griswold, we don't want to be getting all blubbery on the first day of school, do we?"

Freddy shook his head and laughed, his eyes welled up. Mrs. McVicker remembered the camera and fetched it from the butler's pantry. "Mister Charles, would you take a picture of me and Francis? I want to remember this day."

"Smile." Charles said and snapped the picture.

"You don't want to be late on the first day of school." She paused, and then added, "Freddy."

As Freddy got to the doorway he turned around and looked back at Mrs. McVicker, "You called me Freddy."

He felt in his pocket for the Quell Stone. He rubbed it and said to himself, "What is true, what is right, I will be protected." He felt his pocket buzz and tiny golden sparks shot out. "Yeow, hold on cowboy," he muttered as he withdrew his hand and patted the bulge.

His grandmother was reading the newspaper on the divan, looking regal in her red velvet robe and matching slippers.

"Good morning, Grandmother Webbe."

Mrs. Webbe kept her eyes on the paper, ignoring his greeting. "Come here. Let's have a look at you. Your tie's crooked." She reached up and jerked it straight, looked him up and down and said, "Now… listen to me carefully, Francis. You better behave yourself. I will not tolerate any shenanigans from you."

"Yes, Grandmother Webbe."

"That's all." Mrs. Webbe resumed reading the newspaper.

Freddy turned to leave, and then stopped. "Grandmother Webbe, thank you."

Mrs. Webbe looked up startled, "What? Oh. You're welcome." Almost inaudibly she said, "Have a good day, Francis."

Freddy rubbed the Quell Stone for luck, turned, and headed back to the kitchen.

Charles was downing his second cup of coffee, and looked at his watch, "We'd better get going."

Freddy felt a knot in his stomach and became nauseated. He didn't know anyone at Wiggins and wouldn't have anyone to eat lunch with.

*What if I get lost and can't find my classes? What if the teachers are mean?* His legs felt weak.

"Okay Charles," he said, "I guess I'm ready."

"Do you have your class schedule?" Mrs. McVicker asked as she handed Freddy his sack lunch.

"Got it," Freddy said pulling it from his pocket to wave it in the air as he followed Charles out the door.

Charles and Freddy were discussing the latest edition of *Hot Rod* when they pulled up to "The Grand Lady," as Wiggins Prep was affectionately called. The Greco-Roman inspired building was large, commanding, and sitting prominently on the mountainside overlooking St. Wigbod. Semicircular marble steps led to the main entrance. At the top were six granite pillars supporting a pediment and entablature proclaiming the name Wiggins Preparatory. On each side of the steps were brick and terra-cotta trimmed bases holding cast-iron candelabras.

It took Freddy a moment to take it all in. "Whew, it's enormous." He felt a rip of terror.

.

"I told you 'The Lady' was big." Charles exited the car and opened Freddy's door. "You'll do just fine," he said, handing Freddy his book bag. "I'll see you at 3:30. Look for me on Tidewater Street." Charles ruffled Freddy's hair and shut the car door.

Freddy waved and moved apprehensively toward the stairs, his legs heavy. He wished he could disappear. Groups of students were scattered about or screaming greetings at each other.

Freddy looked at his schedule crumpled up in his tight-fisted hand. His stomach was making a growling sound and his bladder felt as if it would explode.

The bell rang. Students began rushing into the building and Freddy found himself being swept along in a tidal wave of bodies. Everywhere he looked, kids were scurrying like mice dodging cats' claws.

Freddy stopped to examine his schedule and was rear ended by a girl in a pleated skirt. Her forest green knee socks barely covered her knobby knees. A green and yellow plaid ribbon was pinned to her tightly curled red hair.

"Sorry," Freddy said.

"My fault," she said. "Wasn't looking where I was going. Mother says if I didn't have my head screwed on

.

tight, it'd roll off and bounce out the door. Geez, you know where the eighth grade wing is?"

"Nope." Freddy said, looking around for a teacher.

An announcement came over the loud speaker. "Eighth graders come to the trophy case in the main hall. All eighth graders report to the trophy case."

Out of the chaos, order began taking place as the eighth grade students headed down the marble hall to the trophy case. Beautifully carved Roman columns rose up to the arched ceiling of the main hall. Standing adjacent to the trophy case was a man holding a bullhorn.

Yelling through the bullhorn, the man said, "Good morning new Wiggies. Welcome! I am Mr. Flowers, music teacher at our prestigious and venerable school that is for the selected few. Many seek our institution but few are chosen."

He stood for a moment as if in meditation.

"You are the best hope for a new generation of Wiggins' leaders. Our motto is 'Wiggie Proud.' Say it softly, say it reverently and say it often. Now Wiggies! Sound out our motto!"

Some students looked at one another, unsure of what to do; others muttered indistinctly.

"Pitiful, pitiful." Mr. Flowers pointed in Freddy's direction. "You! Come here."

Dazed, Freddy looked around and ducked his head. *I hope he's not pointing at me.*

"Yes! You with the rooster tail. Come here."

Students stared at Freddy, and snickered, catcalling "Rooster tail!"

Head down, Freddy stumbled to the trophy case.

"This student will demonstrate how we show our school pride. What's your name?"

Whispering he said, "Freddy."

"Is that your proper name?"

Freddy shook his head. "But everybody calls me Freddy."

Mr. Flowers shook his finger at Freddy and said, "At Wiggins we do not use common nicknames. We show our ancestral pride. What is your Christian name?"

"Francis." *What's the uproar about a nickname?*

"Now, Francis, what is our motto?

Freddy felt his face burn, "Wiggie Proud."

"Too soft," Mr. Flowers said. "Say it loudly with enthusiasm. Now! Say it with pride. Lift your head high. Here, use the bullhorn."

Freddy's face reddened and he swallowed hard. "Wiggie Proud," he said louder.

Satisfied, Mr. Flowers sent Freddy back to the group. *This school is getting weirder and weirder.*

"The eighth grade hall is to my right." Mr. Flowers pointed at two upper classmen... a skinny girl with braids and a chubby boy with glasses. Mr. Flowers turned back to the newcomers. "They will help you find your way around and point you in the right direction," he said. "Okay—get going."

"Don't be late for homeroom," Mr. Flowers said, wiping his brow and glaring at the newcomers. *How ghastly.*

The group thundered down the hall toward their guides.

The eighth grade wing was soon awash with shouts of, "There's my class!" and "I found it!" and "We're in homeroom together!"

At the very end of the hallway Freddy stood in front of room 100, his homeroom class. Freddy eyed the four girls and seven boys lined up against the wall. He wondered if they would be friendly or stuck up. He took his place at the end of the line. Running toward him at top speed was the red headed girl, her bow barely hanging on. "Made it!" she yelled, crashing into Freddy. Freddy was knocked off balance and stumbled into the student in front of him.

THE TARDY BELL RANG!

.

    The students began pushing one another. "Move back!" someone hollered. There was more pushing. A lunch bag was dropped. "Don't step on my lunch!" a boy yelled.

# CHAPTER 9
# THE TEACHERS

Miss Scales appeared at the classroom door, clapping her hands. "Stop! Stop this! What's going on? Get up and get back in line." She stomped her foot. "This is the unruliest bunch of students I have ever witnessed."

Miss Jesylee Scales, stern-faced and bone skinny, appeared taller than her actual five-foot seven-inch frame. She wore a blue and white sailor dress, blue flats, and white stockings. A tiny ribbon-shaped barrette held back her pepper-grey short bob. Rouge filled the many wrinkles in her cheeks. "I expect you to be in line and prepared for learning before the tardy bell rings. I never want to see this type of behavior again."

Miss Scales inhaled and appeared to heighten as she stepped from child to child, scrutinizing each one. She shook her head and sighed. "You may enter. Be seated and wait for my instructions."

Thirteen wide-eyed new Wiggies quietly entered the sanctuary of Miss Jesylee Scales. A bust of Edgar Allen Poe, atop a Roman styled pedestal, stood to the right of her desk. A stuffed raven, wings spread in flight, hung from the ceiling. On the single bulletin board were thumbtacked pictures of Henry Wadsworth Longfellow, Emily Dickenson, John Greenleaf Whittier, Robert Frost, and Carl Sandberg. It was captioned American Poets. Otherwise, the room was devoid of embellishment. The wooden desk-chairs were arranged in semicircular rows.

All students save one took a seat and waited for instructions. A boy sitting beside Freddy began fiddling with a pencil and drumming.

Miss Scales strolled over to the lad. She whispered, "Do you understand English?"

He stopped, and looked up at her. "Uh, huh."

"Obviously you can't speak proper English. 'Uh, huh' is not a word." Miss Scales' voice rose like a tsunami. She glared at the boy, and tapped her foot, "Why did you deliberately ignore my instructions?"

He sunk into his chair. "What instructions?"

"I distinctly remember telling this class to be seated and wait for my instructions. Didn't you hear me say that? Well, did you?"

"I'm s-s-sorry," he stuttered.

"Well then, go to the blackboard and write, 'I will listen to Miss Scales', twenty-five times." She walked back to her desk, and positioned herself against the front panel.

"And what is your name 'Mister I Can't Follow Directions'?"

"A-A-Anthony H- H-Houlgrave."

Miss Scales addressed the class, "I hope you will take a lesson from M-M-Mister H-H-Houlgrave." She picked up the class roster and cleared her throat. "I will now call roll.

Please raise your hand and say 'present'. Carly Archer."

Raising her hand, "Present."

"Edward Brinto."

"Here," he said, hands supporting his cheeks, eyes cast down.

Miss Scales' eyes narrowed, her mouth twitched. "Mr. Brinto, go to the back of the room and face the wall."

Eddie Brinto took his time collecting his things and sauntered to the back of the class where he sat facing the wall.

The next four students answered roll properly— Eustace Clovill, Roger Cooke, Anne Dixon and Robert Ford.

"Erin Frith," Miss Scales said.

No answer.

"Erin Frith," she said again.

.

"Oh, sorry Miss Scales, present," Erin said, raising her hand, her red bangs covering her eyes. "My mother said to tell you hello. She said she missed you at church…"

Miss Scales glared. "That kind of inattention will not do at Wiggins. Stop blathering. And… do not think you will get special favors because your grandfather is on the Board of Education."

Erin's face turned red, she swallowed a gulp of air and her lip quivered.

The barrette holding Miss Scales' mousy hair came loose. She unsnapped it and threw it on the desk. "If there is no objection from the peanut gallery I will continue…"

"Francis Griswold, Edgar Harrington."    Each answered roll to Miss Scales' satisfaction.

"Anthony Houlgrave."

From the blackboard, Tony stuttered, "P-P-Present."

Miss Scales briefly glanced at Tony and smiled with genuine satisfaction. "Molly Martin." She continued, "John Stevenson."

Wearing a smug smile and sitting perfectly erect, John's hand shot up, "Present, Miss Scales."

Miss Scales took note of this young man.

"And last but not least, Kendall Waller."

Smiling, displaying her perfectly straight teeth, Kendall raised her hand and said, "Present, Miss Scales."

Miss Scales smiled, revealing her crooked front teeth, "At least I have two students worthy of the first row of my class."

Miss Jesylee Scales had been teaching English at Wiggins for twenty-six years. In four more years she would be eligible to retire. She never married and was not fond of children. The highlight of her day was between classes when she visited with history teacher, Mr. Kendall Gore, her next door neighbor.

The crackle of the intercom broke the silence in room 100. "Attention all students! This is Principal Hister. I want to welcome all students back for another year of learning and Wiggie Pride. Our credo at Wiggins is 'Knowledge, Wisdom, and Maturity.' Your teachers are prepared to give you the knowledge to gain wisdom and maturity. You will be successful at Wiggins if you give your best effort every day. Your homeroom teachers will now hand out the updated schedules. Be on time to each class and prepared to learn."

An ear-splitting squeal came from the intercom. "Go Wiggins! Wiggie Pride!" Mr. Hister shouted, and signed off.

While Miss Scales handed out schedules, Erin placed a neatly folded note on Freddy's desk. He stared at

.

the paper, then glanced at Erin who was mouthing, "Open it."

Freddy covered the note with his right hand, slid it over the top of his desk, and cautiously opened it underneath. Freddy's face flushed reading its contents. "Hi, Francis! Want to eat lunch together?" A small heart dotted the *i* of Erin's florid signature.

Miss Scales moved near Freddy and said "Let me have it."

"Have what?" Freddy's voice cracked.

"The note under your desk," Miss Scales demanded.

Sheepishly, Freddy handed it over. Miss Scales read the note and said, "There will be no note writing in my class. Those who choose to disobey will eat their lunch in this room and copy *The Declaration of Independence*. Looking at Erin and Freddy, Miss Scales said, "You two are fortunate because I do not enforce punishment until the second day of school."

Freddy was thinking. *This place is like a reform school. You wiggle a finger and get busted.*

Miss Scales handed Freddy his schedule, keeping the note. The bell rang, marking the end of homeroom.

Erin materialized beside Freddy. "Sorry you got in trouble."

"Now I'm on Scales' bad side and she will have it in for me, thanks to you," Freddy said

Erin was keeping abreast of Freddy, "So, do you?"

"Do what?"

"Want to eat lunch with me," Erin said, her red curls bouncing.

"Yeah, I guess…let's see." Freddy's pace quickened. Searching for the boy's restroom, he spotted one near the main hall. "Gotta go."

Freddy swept past two boys coming out and his schedule slipped out of his hand and dropped onto the wet floor, soaking up liquid from around the urinal. *Good grief! I'm not picking that up.* He dropped a paper towel over the wet schedule and kicked the wad behind the trash can.

Freddy remembered his old schedule stashed in his book bag, and found it crumpled but dry. Next class – history.

Freddy moved through the hall. The door to room 101 was closed; the door locked. Freddy peered through the glass-framed door at Mr. Gore's back. The students were focused on the teacher. Soon one student after another pointed at the door.

THE TARDY BELL RANG!

Mr. Gore turned to the door his eyes magnified by the coke-bottle sized lenses in his black framed glasses. He tried to open the door but realized someone had turned the lock. "This door is to remain open," he muttered as he unlocked the door.

Mr. Gore cracked open the door. "You're late, sir. Excuse or reason?"

"I was in the bathroom and dropped my schedule in water. This older boy grabbed it, crumpled it up and threw it in the trash," Freddy hated to lie. "I had to fish it out."

"Do you have it?"

"What?"

"Your wet schedule."

Crumpled in his fist, Freddy held out his old schedule. "Humm...doesn't feel wet. Guess things dry pretty fast around here. Don't be tardy for class unless you get a tardy pass."

"It won't happen again, sir."

"Take that empty chair on the front row."

Freddie grimaced when Erin smiled and gestured to the chair next to hers.

Today, as with every day, Mr. Kendall Gore was wearing beige—beige pants, shirt, socks, and necktie. He told his colleagues it was easier to have everything one color. He could sleep as late as possible, pull out a shirt and pants and be coordinated.  A solitary man, he had been married briefly when he was twenty-one after graduating from college.  His bride of three weeks told him she could not tolerate his boring personality and was not cut out for married life.  She called a cousin in Garden City, California, bought a bus ticket and headed west. After that, the only contact Gore had with her was via her lawyer annulling their marriage.

Mr. Gore stepped to the center of the room, yardstick in hand.  He cleared his throat. "Welcome, one and all."  As he spoke, his head bobbled— his peculiar affliction.  He called roll; his head bobbled.  He walked to the blackboard; his head bobbled.  It was intriguing and at the same time, painful to watch. Mr. Gore positioned himself in the middle of the room. "American history is fascinating," he said. "Some describe our country's beginning in contradictory terms. *Revolutionary or cruel betrayal*-- *Heroic patriots or cowardly traitors* But, I say to you that every man, and every body of men on earth, possesses the right of self government." Mr. Gore's voice rose and fell like surf water hitting the beach.  He walked to the back of the room and pulled up the window.  Fresh cool morning air circulated and Freddy turned in his seat.

Raising the yardstick high, Mr. Gore's voice rose with fervor. "Mankind is governed more by feelings than by reason." He ended his theatrics with a bobbling nod of his head.

Freddy counted five head bobbles. In the row behind him, John Stevenson made a goon face, rolling his eyes and bobbling his head. Freddy resisted the urge to burst out laughing. He turned back to face the front of the room and caught Eddie Brinto sticking a wad of gum under his desk.

Mr. Gore pounded the yardstick on the oak floor. Heads turned. "You have an assignment. I have just quoted from two of our most prodigious founding fathers." He crisscrossed the rows, tapping each desk he passed with the yardstick and arrived at the blackboard at the front of the class. He pulled up the map and uncovered the quotes he had just recited. "You will be detectives…read pages one to twenty in search of clues. Find the authors of these prophetic quotes. Then answer the questions at the end of the chapter. This is your assignment. Begin."

Mr. Gore pulled out the desk chair, sat down, and surveyed his new pupils. Freddy counted seven more head bobbles.

There was hustle and bustle as students unzipped their book bags, pulled out paper, and pencil, and their history books. Soon heads were buried in those books.

Someone sneezed.

"Bless you," a voice whispered.

Another sneeze. Another "bless you". A snicker and a giggle followed.

Head bobbling, Mr. Gore said, "Get to work!"

A bee-like buzz was heard from the back. With heads and eyes lowered, Carly Archer and Anne Dixon burst out in gales of laughter.

Mr. Gore stood up, his magnified eyes glaring, "Talking will cease!"

"There're bees in the room!" Eddie Brinto yelled. "They're swarming!"

Kids jumped out of their seats, swatting and screaming. Mr. Gore ran to the door and into the hall yelling, "Bees. Get the janitor. I'm allergic."

Pandemonium filled the classroom. John Stevenson grabbed Erin's hair and pulled her bow off. Erin kicked him on the shin. John grabbed his leg and fell to the floor moaning.

Freddy squatted next to John, offering him a hand up. "Get away from me," John said.

The janitor burst into the classroom armed with a can of wasp spray. Mr. Gore followed, surveying the destroyed classroom. "Where're the bees?"

Seeing John Stevenson on the floor, Mr. Gore said, "Who did this?" John pointed to Freddy.

Mr. Gore glared at Freddy. "Mr. Griswold, you are not getting off to a good start. First, you're late to class and now you've kicked a student down. You may get expelled from our institution before you get started. I want you to write a 25-word essay on The Importance of Civility in our Society. Hand it in when you enter class tomorrow."

The bell rang ending first period.

John Stevenson caught up to Erin in the hall. "Wanna hear a joke?

"No!"

"Confucius say red-headed girl have brown hair by cracky," John pushed Erin, laughed in her face and ran down the hall.

"You're despicable!" Erin shouted, rubbing her shoulder.

Freddy was lingering in the hall reviewing his schedule when Erin approached and yanked the paper out of his hand, "We've got math together."

Freddy grabbed his schedule back, "I'm not stupid…quit being so obnoxious."

"Oh, excuse me, Francis."

"FREDDY! I go by Freddy." He turned to the left noticing the classroom numbers getting larger.

"It's down this way," Erin said, plodding along beside Freddy. "I hear Mr. Profit is strict. He smells like cigarettes…Yuck."

Across from the teacher's lounge was room 124. The hall was foul-smelling. Freddy stopped to get a drink of water and Erin headed into the classroom. Entering the room Freddy noticed Erin sitting on the front row and whisked past her. He took a seat next to Tony.

Erin dug around in her book bag. She turned around waving a CarPop. "I got a '57 Chevy."

Bobby Ford, Edgar Harrington, and Eddie Brinto jumped out of their seats and rushed toward Erin. "I'll trade you," Eddie said, grabbing at the coveted candy.

Erin popped the sugary delicacy in her mouth. "Delicious!"

Across the hall, the door to the teachers' lounge opened, belching out a cloud of smoke. Mr. Profit entered room 124 looking like a drill sergeant, slammed his briefcase on the worn-out desk, and turned to the class. Arms folded across his chest, he eyed the new matriculates and waited.

"Shush…shush…shush…shhhhh!" Erin said.

Eddie Brinto looked startled and returned to his seat followed by Edgar and Bobby.

Mr. Profit prided himself in the fear he instilled. Few tested him. Known for being a no-nonsense teacher, he spoke in clipped phrases, and kept his class fast-paced. He drilled mathematical concepts into his pupils until they got it.

Profit unlocked the case and removed a metal ruler and timer. All eyes were focused on the balding instructor as he placed the ruler on the desk and called roll. He set the timer and began writing on the blackboard in scientific notation while explaining mathematical concepts. Five minutes later he turned to his students. "Any questions?"

Silence. Timidly, Erin raised her hand half-way. "Sir, you're going too fast."

"Really? I assumed you must know everything because of the disorder and lollygagging when I entered. Anyone else think I'm going too fast?"

Hands began to raise. "I see." He reached for the ruler aiming it at the students. "To act is easy...to think is hard." He slapped the ruler against his palm. "When you enter the classroom, you will sit, take out your textbook, notebook paper and be ready for mathematics."

Mr. Profit handed out a five-page review exam to the grumbling students and set the timer. "You have twenty minutes."

Mr. Profit walked out into the hall and talked to another teacher.

John Stevenson got up to sharpen his pencil and on his way back snatched the timer.

Freddy scanned the first page, and drew a blank. He gripped his pencil with too much force, breaking the lead. While Freddy was sharpening his pencil, John put the timer under Freddy's desk.

Freddy heard furious scribbling and rustling of pages. His heart pounded in his chest…surely others could hear it. *Calm down. Breathe.*

He glanced at Tony who seemed to be stuck on the first problem.

The directions stated, *"Read all the way through the test before working any problems."*

So Freddy re-read the directions, and scanned the test to the end, and looked over problem number 50. It read, *"Congratulations! You have successfully followed directions. Now only complete problems 48 and 49."*

He smiled and quickly solved the two simple problems and placed his pencil in the groove on the desk.

Mr. Profit reentered the classroom, noticing his timer was gone. He scanned the room. "Which one of you knot heads took my timer?" he growled.

Students began searching. John Stevenson announced, "It's under Frances' desk, sir."

Mr. Profit faced Freddy, "Get out in the hall, funny boy."

Bewildered, Freddy said, "Sir, I don't know how the timer got under my desk, honest." Freddy thought about it. *I bet it was John, he seems like the type that'd get his jollies seeing other kids get in trouble.*

Mr. Profit reached for a paddle from behind his desk. "This is the Board of Education," he said slapping the paddle on his palm. "You get to meet the Board up close and personal when you act up in my class. Come on, Griswold."

The classroom got deathly silent. They heard a loud whack. Mr. Profit came back into the classroom, put the paddle away and continued as if nothing unusual had happened. Freddy followed, sat down, and put his head on his desk. *At least Profit doesn't give hard licks. I've got to get away from this chamber of horrors.* Then a vision of his mother floated through him mind.

"Times up! Pass your tests forward."

Students voiced their protests. John Stevenson cried, "My parents will murder me."

Mr. Profit stood at the door of his classroom thumbing through the tests, checking the last page. He looked at Freddy as he was leaving the classroom, "Well, at least you're not stupid."

Eustace Clovill and Eddie Brinto stepped in front of Freddy, blocking his way in the hall. "Hey man, does your butt hurt?" Eustace said, his breath smelling of cigarettes.

"Who put that timer under my desk?" Freddy asked.

Eustace shrugged his shoulders, "I didn't see anything. I was taking that stupid test."

"Oh, sure. See no evil.... Know where the music room is at?" Freddy said.

Eustace said. "Downstairs near the cafeteria. You can smell it." Eustace looked at Eddie for approval, chuckling at his own joke.

"Good one, Spiderman," Eddie said.

The three boys pushed through a clump of giggling girls at the end of the eighth grade wing. Black marble steps led to the ground floor. At the bottom Freddy turned left, spotted Mr. Flowers heaving along as Eustace and Eddie raced past.

At the end of the long hallway was a glassed-in room containing risers, a piano and folding chairs arranged in rows of four. One side of the room faced Tidewater Street at ground level. Seven floor-to-ceiling double-hung sash windows provided the light source for the music room.

A ledge swept along the entire battery of windows making it a suitable perch for birds and other creatures.

Freddy entered the music room, selected a seat by Tony and dropped his book bag. Eustace and Eddie slumped in their chairs at the rear; Eustace was cleaning his fingernails with a paperclip. Seated on the first row, Carly Archer and Anne Dixon looked into their compacts and applied lipstick. Next to them, Molly Martin was reading *The Good Earth.* John Stevenson and Kendall Waller climbed on the riser playing tag. Bobby Ford, Edgar Harrington and Roger Cooke stood at the windows looking out. Edgar struggled to open a window. Bobby and Roger joined in and they fully raised it. Bobby climbed out onto the ledge and beckoned for Edgar and Roger to join him. Edgar obliged and the two boys jumped off the ledge onto the grass below. They wiggled and twisted, their arms raised and waving.

Fearing the class would get into trouble, Freddy ran to the door and looked out, "Flowers is coming." Roger pulled the window shut, jumped into the nearest seat and folded his hands on his desk.

Freddy raced back to his chair.

Mr. Flowers entered the music room huffing and puffing. A portly fifty-two year old man, George Flowers was wearing baggy grey slacks, and a rumpled tan sports jacket. His tie was loose; one end flapped over his shoulder. This was his first year at Wiggins and his first year to teach. Before this, his job was playing trumpet for "The King of Jazz" Paul Whiteman and his orchestra. His music credentials were first rate but he was out of his league at Wiggins. This morning someone in his first period had turned over the trash can spilling its contents into the hall.

Mr. Flowers headed to the piano, pulled out a handkerchief from his satchel and wiped his brow. Red faced and still breathing hard, he watched John and Kendall playing on the riser. "You two get down and take a seat," he said.

Erin entered class as the tardy bell rang dropping the armful of books she was carrying. "Oh geez, this just isn't my day," she said. John Stevenson jumped off the riser to help Erin pick up her books.

Mr. Flowers poured himself a glass of water, gulped it down and belched. "Everyone to your seat!" He called the roll, noting the absence of Robert Ford and Edgar Harrington. Erin glanced at the window as Mr. Flowers was putting the attendance slip on the wall clip.

"Mr. Flowers," Erin said, "Bobby and Edgar are outside!"

"Oh, for crying out loud," he said spitting his words out. He motioned to Freddy, "Open the window…"

Bobby and Edgar re-entered the classroom, heads down like scolded puppies.

Mr. Flowers pointed to the door and yelled, "Out…get out…"

"Where to?" Bobby whined.

"I don't care…just get out of my classroom."

Pulling a tall stool to the front of the class, Mr. Flowers plopped his bottom down devouring the seat, one foot on the bottom rung. He pulled out a handkerchief from his back pocket, wiped his brow, blew his nose, cleared his throat, reached for another gulp of water and said, "I have come to Wiggins Preparatory to impart my love of music to you. I have some exciting plans. Number one: Starting an orchestra that will be the absolute envy of every other school. We'll have a choir for those who love to sing. This is your chance to be a part of an awesome musical experience."

Checking his roster, he looked at Carly Archer, and said, "Miss Archer put the lipstick away."

Blushing with embarrassment, Carly put the cosmetic away.

"Are there any questions?"

Eustace cocked his head, "Yeah, like I really like Fats Domino and Elvis. We gonna do some Blueberry Hill?"

"Actually, Mr. Antoine 'Fats' Domino is a great boogie-woogie piano player. He puts a New Orleans-style spin on rock and roll and oooh does he sing some smooth rhythm & blues....oh, yes. I did a gig with him a few years back at the Hideaway Club in New Orleans."

Freddy was sitting up listening to every word.

"What's Fats like?" Eustace blurted.

"Can you get him to come to our school?" Kendall said. "Our first sock-hop is coming up in October? I'm in charge of entertainment."

"Do you teach boogie-woogie piano?" Freddie asked.

"Okay, okay!! Listen up. We've got to get class started. Those of you interested in orchestra, singing in the choir or boogie-woogie," Flowers glanced at Freddy, "stay after class."

The eleven new Wiggies then practiced sitting up straight, breathing from the diaphragm and singing scales.

The lunch bell rang, but Freddy stayed after class and signed up for piano lessons on Tuesdays after school.

Freddy entered the cafeteria through the double swinging doors. *This place smells like rotten fish. How can anyone eat in here without throwing up?* Looking around, he didn't see anyone he knew. Feeling alone and completely out of place, Freddy guessed he would have to eat by himself.

On his right was the full service lunch line. Beefy ladies dressed in white uniforms, black hairnets and white nurse's shoes placed a corndog, corn niblets, fried potatoes, ketchup and rice pudding onto each plate. Along the wall an ice cooler held pint-sized containers of white or chocolate milk. The greasy smell of deep fried food permeated the air. The area was stuffy and humid from the steam spray and body heat.

The noise of squealing laughter was deafening. Rectangular tables placed throughout the cafeteria held from six to eight students. Freddy drifted by the table where John, Kendall, Carly and Anne were seated.

"Do you mind if I sit with you guys?" Freddy said looking at John and feeling a jab of uncertainty.

"It depends," John smirked. "Tell you what, Kimosabe. If you can answer this question you can join our group. It's really very simple…. Are you a turtle?"

"Desert or water turtle?" Freddy said.

The students at John's table exploded in laughter. "Sorry, Rooster, that's not the answer," John said. "I guess you'll have to eat by yourself."

"Freddy, over here," someone called through cupped hands. Freddy scanned the tables and saw Erin and Tony. Erin was waving him over. Freddy smiled and joined them.

"Are you going to be in band?" Erin said, crunching on a carrot. "Mama said I have to develop my musical talents. Maybe I should sing...I don't know. What do you think?"

Freddy unzipped his book bag and pulled out a brown paper sack. "Do what you like."

"What are you going to take?"

"I don't know. Maybe piano...boogie-woogie."

"Me too!" Tony said, and began punching out chords on the table. "I found my thri-ill, on Blueberry Hi-ill..."

"Cool, dude," Freddy said, joining in.

He opened his lunch sack and found a folded note that read, *'Hope your day is as great as you are,* Mrs. M.'

He smiled and took out a ham sandwich, sliced apples and four oatmeal raisin cookies. For the first time in hours he thought of his Quell Stone. He patted his pocket and felt a slight rumble. *I wonder if my Quell Stone could make John vanish or turn into a turtle.*

Freddy stood up and dug in his pocket for a nickel. He grabbed some chocolate milk from the cooler and sat back down next to Tony. "I love cold milk" Freddy said, gulping the entire contents at once.

He glanced around the room. "What's with John, anyway?

"He's a s-s-suck-up." Tony said.

Erin pulled out her last carrot. "Mama says his mother's a drunk. He'll probably turn out the same way."

Freddy crushed his lunch sack into a ball. "John asked me if I was a turtle. Know what means?"

"Don't know," Erin said, "but I think it's a code for their stupid club."

Sounds of chairs scooting back on the tile floor, the clanking of dishes being dumped in the dirty dish area signaled lunchtime was drawing to a close.

Freddy, Tony, and Erin strolled out to the front of the school, book bags in tow, and leaned up against a column. The entire city was visible; a cool refreshing breeze soothed their moist skin.

John, and his posse passed Freddy and his friends and he pointed his finger at Freddy, "Hey dude, are you a turtle?"

"Are you?" Freddy said.

Kendall and Anne replied in unison, "Bet your sweet ass he is."

"That's good information to have." Freddy said, "I'll have to remember that."

The bell rang. End of lunch.

"I know where the science room is. Follow me." Erin walked forward confidently. Tony and Freddy lagged behind. Erin turned around, and pulled Tony by the arm, "Come on!"

"Erin, you're not my m-m-mother," Tony protested.

"You need one. You would be late for your funeral if I wasn't here. Mama says you only have one chance to make a good first impression."

Tony whispered to Freddy, "How do we get rid of her?"

Freddy shrugged, "I don't know. I think we're stuck with her."

The science lab was located on the second floor between the girls' and the boys' bathrooms. An eight foot transomed door led into the oversized room, home to ten science tables each equipped with a sink, a tall water faucet, and a Bunsen burner. A cabinet underneath the sink housed the water pipes and hoses for gas. Along the wall nearest the hall, were containers of test tubes, scales, measuring cups, cotton balls, spoons and safety goggles. An open closet revealed jars and dusty bottles of chemicals. In his white lab coat, Mr. Studley, unaware of the students in the hall, was staring into a microscope making notations on a pad. He held a slide up to the light, placed it under the microscope and adjusted the focus. The tardy bell rang.

Freddy waited with the rest of the science class in the hall for some sign to enter. Edward turned to Freddy. "Is he deaf?"

"Roger, drop your books," Eustace said.

Mr. Studley looked at his watch and then the door. "Oh …didn't hear the bell. Come in. Find your nameplate and be seated. "

Freddy found his name at the same table where Carly was sitting. Freddy smiled at the thought of the prettiest girl in eighth grade as his lab partner. Freddy saw Tony's partner. He stifled a laugh. *Poor guy. Got stuck with Erin.*

Mr. Studley handed out lab manuals with the safety rules. One by one each was read aloud. Students practiced putting on safety goggles, their lab coats, and watched a demonstration of how to operate the eye wash station in case chemicals got in their eyes. Mr. Studley showed off the scar on the back of his hand, the result of an acid spill; he had assumed the bottle cap was screwed on tight.

At the end of the demonstration, Mr. Studley paired up the lab partners telling them to write down the rules from memory. Carly leaned close to Freddy, her black hair brushing the side of his face. His hands began to sweat. He pressed too hard on his pencil and the lead broke. He checked around for the pencil sharpener. On the way to the sharpener he noticed water dripping from the eye wash station. He reached to tighten the handle and water sprayed out on his head. Frantically, he turned the handle but more water gushed out. An arm pushed him aside and the deluge stopped. Droplets of water streamed down Freddy's face.

"This is exactly the kind of thing I was just talking about. A science room is a catastrophe waiting to happen. I don't want to have to call your parents and tell them you lost an eye or something worse."

Freddy's new Weejuns were soaked. Pointing to the door, Mr. Studley said, "Better get dried off." He threw Freddy a towel. Freddy's skin tingled as he passed his lab partner. The water squishing out of his shoes sounded like an old rusty door needing oil.

The bell rang. Science was over.

The boys raced out of science class down three flights of stairs to the basement locker room. The girls reported to the gym.

Coach Benjamin Beast stood six-foot four-inches tall in his official Wiggins' Physical Education uniform— a navy blue crested tee shirt, yellow shorts, navy socks and white high top Converse tennis shoes. He worked out with weights and was proud of his twenty-inch neck and large biceps which had earned him his nickname 'The Beast'.

The boys were assigned lockers and told to take their gym clothes home on Fridays to be washed. Anyone not properly dressed out couldn't participate that day, would receive a zero, and be required to do 25 pushups.

"You have five minutes to suit up and report to the field," Coach Beast yelled, his voice gravelly and hoarse.

Freddy forgot to bring his P.E. clothes and had to do pushups. Coach Beast lectured him on the importance of physical education. *Maybe my grandmother was right that I can't make it at Wiggins.* Then he saw a vision of his mother saying, "You can do it. Believe in yourself."

The boys huddled around Coach Beast. All he wanted them to do was run one mile…four times around the track. They lined up across the track. The whistle blew.

John Stevenson shot off like a rocket then threw up halfway into the first lap. Eustace, Bobby, and Edgar managed two laps before falling out. Tony and Roger were side by side into the fourth lap. Roger, gasping for air, kept going.

His heart pounding, Tony felt the burn in his legs. Out of his peripheral vision he saw Roger pushing ahead. Tony caught his second wind, passed Roger and finished first. The two boys stumbled over to the grass.

Tony doubled over inhaling frantically for air.

Freddy did five pushups before collapsing. *Wow, I am so out of shape.*

Coach Beast told the boys that they were all miserable wimps and that he was going to whip them into shape. He blew his whistle and said, "Okay, hit the showers. You've got 10 minutes,"

Freddy caught up to Tony. "You gonna shower?" Freddy asked apprehensively.

"Yea, I g-guess w-we have to. The B- B-Beast will be checking."

Freddy said, "What if I go hide out? I don't want to get naked in front of a bunch of guys." He could feel himself beginning to hyperventilate. He remembered his Quell Stone. He took it out and rubbed it over and over. Silver and gold sparks showered the air. A calm feeling blanketed Freddy and his fear began to lighten.

The shower room was all steamed up when Freddy entered. Self consciously Freddy took off his shoes and socks. He took a step back and slipped on a bar of soap and fell on his rear. Heads peeked around the shower stalls and the boys began laughing and cat calling.

Coach Beast heard the commotion and rushed in. "What's going on in here?" he blasted.

"Francis fell on his butt," John said laughing. "What a butt head."

"Cut the name calling, Stevenson. You've just earned one demerit. Three and you'll be feeling my Board of Education," Coach Beast said to John with disgust.

"Go to the nurse, and let her check you out," Coach said, helping Freddy up.

Freddy limped away rubbing his behind, feeling embarrassed and defeated. "What could possibly get worse?" He mumbled to himself. *At least 'Turtle John' got some of his own medicine.*

# Chapter 10
# Principal's Office

Even though he was still feeling the sting of his fall, Freddy was the first in line outside room 100. The girls filed in behind. Tony had a slight limp. John was in the nurses' office complaining of stomach cramps. The last boys to arrive were red faced, shirts untucked, ties loose, and they were rubbing various aching limbs.

At her classroom door, Miss Jesylee Scales glowered at the students. "Someone reeks of pig's feet," she said while holding her neatly pressed handkerchief over her nose.

Behind Freddy, Erin whispered, "You've got hair on your chinny, chin, chin."

The more he thought of what she said, he was overcome with the giggles and he snorted. *Erin cracks me up.* A symphony of pig snorts and grunts rang forth from the class.

"Francis Griswold," Miss Scales shrieked, "go to the office and don't come back until you can act civilized!"

Freddy hobbled down the corridor of the eighth grade wing, turned right into the main hall and found the swinging doors that said Office. Pushing open the doors, Freddy was face to face with Mrs. Blackstone, the school secretary. She peered at him through her red rhinestone-studded cat-eyed glasses. *This is not going to go well.* "Miss Scales told me to come to the office," he stuttered.

"Why?"

"I laughed."

"You laughed at Miss Scales?"

Freddy shook his head. "Miss Scales said something funny and the girl behind me said something funny...I tried not to."

Mrs. Blackstone removed her glasses and let them dangle from their glittery chord. Her eyes narrowed to small slits as she asked, "Where's your form?"

"Miss Scales didn't give me anything."

Her raspy voice became shrill. "For the love of Mike! Must I do everything?" She threw her hands up in disgust.

"Name?"

"Freddy Griswold."

She pointed to the wooden chairs lined up against the wall. "Sit and I'll try to locate your information card. I wouldn't be laughing anymore if I were you."

Freddy gazed out into the foyer, and focused on the school mascot, Regit, a full-sized stuffed Bengal tiger. It was rumored that he came to life and stalked the hallowed halls whenever Wiggins beat their arch rival, St. Anthony Academy.

"We don't seem to have a Freddy Griswold enrolled at our institute. Are you sure that is your proper name?"

"Actually, it's Francis, but everyone calls me Freddy,"

"We do not use nicknames at Wiggins Preparatory, Mr. Griswold," Mrs. Blackstone snapped. She filled out the form, stood, straightened her red wool skirt, and disappeared down the hall.

Freddy looked up at the ceiling, studied his hands, and then remembered the Quell Stone. He reached in his pocket and rubbed it.

Mrs. Blackstone, holding a steaming cup of coffee returned to her wide oak desk. She took a sip, set it down, and peered at Freddy. "He's not in a good mood today."

From beyond, came a loud monotone, "Send in Griswold."

Freddy felt faint, his heart beat rapidly, and his mouth was cotton ball dry. When Freddy stood, his feet seemed anchored to the floor. Each step was like wading in molasses. He rubbed the Quell Stone. "I will be protected," he said to himself. A vibration and spark reassured him.

Mrs. Blackstone adjusted her glasses. "Good luck…you'll need it."

The hallway to Mr. Hister's office was long, and narrow. *Geez! This must be what it's like when you're getting executed.*

Freddy paused at the door, squinted at the bright afternoon light streaming through the window and focused on a stringy-haired, pencil thin man in a gray-green suit that matched his skin color. Seated behind an enormous ebony desk, his long legs stretched to the side; he exposed small baked bean teeth through thin gray lips. Dry spittle caked the corners of his mouth.

"Griswold?" Mr. Hister said. He spoke in a drawl, drawing out the syllables.

"Yes, sir."

Mr. Hister studied the discipline form, taking his time. He tapped the form on the desk and motioned for Freddy to come into his office. "Take that chair," he said, pointing to a small desk chair.

Mr. Hister interlaced his fingers except for the indices which he tapped together. "Trouble maker, are you?"

Freddy felt sweat dripping off his forehead. "No sir."

"Well this says you've been making fun of Miss Scales—our best English teacher."

"I wouldn't say that," Freddy's voice trembled.

"So you're saying she's just making all this up?" Mr. Hister rose from his contoured leather chair and extended himself to his full height of six foot two and one half inches. "I don't like your attitude, boy. When you address me you say, yes sir, Mr. Hister."

Freddy's eyes glazed over, "Yes sir, Mr. Hister, sir."

Mr. Hister again studied the card in his hand. "You're new here, aren't you?"

"Yes, sir, Mister Hister," Freddy croaked.

Opening his desk drawer, Hister took out a manual and flipped the pages. Reading from the book, he said "The punishment for your infraction is a day in the dungeon."

Freddy rubbed the Quell Stone hoping it would rescue him. Thoughts of his mother and her loving care flashed through his mind. "Give me another chance, Mr. Hister, sir." Freddy said, his eyes pleading.

"Why should I? These are the rules and rules must be followed."

.

Freddy put his hands together and said, "Sir, I didn't realize. I'm new here…My mother's in the hospital and…" Freddy's eyes welled up.

Mr. Hister tapped the form on the desk. "One chance, boy. I'm sending you back to class and I don't want to ever see you in this office again. But if you are stupid enough to find yourself in trouble again, I will have no choice but to send you down there. Are we clear on this, Griswold?"

"Yes sir, Mr. Hister,"

"Now, git on back to class."

"Thank you, sir."

Freddy gripped his Quell Stone, pulled it out of his pocket, kissed it and said, "Thank you. You just saved my life."

\*\*\*\*\*\*

As Freddy turned into the eighth grade wing, the rancid smell of cigarette smoke hit him in the face. The door to the teachers' lounge closed behind Mr. Profit. *I guess he's having a nicotine fit.*

With each step Freddy felt more anxious. He turned into the boy's bathroom; his bladder was about to explode.

An older boy was combing his hair and admiring himself in the mirror. Then he stuck the comb in his back pocket and sauntered out.

Freddy paced. *Mama always told me not to be afraid of anything that can't eat you. Well, I don't think Miss Scales can eat me so I'll just march on back into that classroom and* ...His stomach churned with nausea. Freddy made it to a stall before heaving. He flushed the toilet, wiped his face with a wet paper towel and looked at himself in the mirror. His rooster tail was sticking up. He doused water on his head and patted the willful hairs into submission.

Reaching into his pocket, Freddy rubbed the smooth stone, left the bathroom and was soon at the door of room 100. He inhaled deeply, spotted an empty seat in the second row and tiptoed in. Tony Houlgrave was at the front of the class stammering and stuttering as he gave a personal introduction speech.

"Mr. Griswold," Miss Scales said, interrupting Tony. "Sit in the back of the class with the rest of your ilk." She turned her attention back to Tony. "Continue your pitifully inadequate presentation, Mr. Houlgrave," she said as her lips twisted in a subtle smirk.

In her classroom, the front row was reserved for her pets and students she deemed worthy. She seated the rest of the class according to her perceived expectations of their ability. At the very back were the hopeless troublemakers. The only way to move out of the back row was to butter her up and to bring her a box of her favorite chocolate pecan caramel candy.

"Sit down, Mr. Houlgrave. We don't have all day." Tony sighed, eyes to the floor and returned to his seat.

The bell rang. End of the day.

Miss Scales instructed the class in the dismissal routine. Students filed past her, row by row. As Freddy passed, she grabbed his arm with her bony, goose-fleshed hand, "I'm afraid you have but one more chance to clear your reputation with me. Your grandmother would be very disappointed to hear of your foolhearty behavior. I like chocolates… Turtles. Just a word to the wise."

Out in the hallway Freddy looked up and down trying to figure out which way to go when Tony Houlgrave approached. "Can you b-b-believe that old b-b-bag Scales? Tony stuttered.

"Oh —my— gosh," Freddy enunciated. "Why would someone who enjoys torturing kids be allowed to teach?"

Tony said, "I've heard she lives here and roams the halls at night looking for signs of her lost love who was killed on their wedding day. This place really is haunted, you know." Tony unzipped his book bag and began rummaging through mounds of crumpled pieces of notebook paper. "Where's that map? No, that's not it...not it...nope...here's my report card from last year. Okay. Here we go," Tony said as he held up a torn crumpled parchment-like paper. "Freddy, this is dynamite — very privileged information."

"Yeah? Hey listen...I'll look at it later. I gotta go. Charles is waitin' for me."

Tony stuffed everything back into his book bag. The two boys walked to the exit leading out onto Tidewater Street. Freddy felt the weight of the world on his back. He was exhausted and this was just the first day of school.

Parked along the curb of Tidewater Street was Grandmother Webbe's black limo. Charles, decked out in gray livery, hopped, came around to the backseat passenger's side, opened it and stood at attention for Freddy. Freddy felt his face burn. As he glanced around, kids were getting into regular cars like two-toned Buicks, Fords, and Chevrolets. Freddy ducked into the car and slid down in the seat. He prayed no one saw him.

Charles went around to the driver's side, and started the engine. He slowly pulled away from the curb. "So, how was your first day?"

"Get outta here," Freddy yelled.

"Hey, Francis? What's the problem?"

"For one thing call me Freddy. FREDDY! And then another thing, couldn't you pick me up about two blocks from school?"

"I guess I could," Charles said, "but you'd have to hightail it like crazy. No messing around. If you're late and keep me waiting then all bets are off. You hear what I'm saying?"

"Thanks, Charles." Freddy got off the floorboard, slumped down into the seat and let out a sigh.

"So Freddy, as I was saying, how did it go?"

"It couldn't have been worse. I did something wrong and got in trouble in every single class. It seemed like I had a sign on my forehead saying, 'Kick me, I'm a trouble maker'."

Charles laughed, "Don't worry, it'll get better. You're the new kid. They just don't know they've got a jewel in their midst."

"I hope so," Freddy said wistfully. Daydreaming, he saw a vision of his mom calling to him. She was trying to tell him something. It seemed like she was saying *"you'll be alright."* He wanted to see her and touch her but she vanished in a wisp. Freddy sat in contemplation but was abruptly jolted back to reality. He rubbed his eyes and shook his head "Oh wow! I could see Mama!"

Charles said, "I guess you were having a daydream."

"It was so real."

Freddy scrounged around in his backpack looking for a CarPop. He popped one in his mouth. "Umm, blueberry. My favorites are candy apple Corvettes, though."

"No way! The sweetest are strawberry '57 Chevys. Ab-so-lute-ly!"

"Mama loves pink bubblegum flavored T-birds," he said sadly. "I hope she's getting better."

"It's hard being away from your Mom, huh?" Charles glanced back at Freddy, his eyes now closed. "My mom passed when I was a baby" Charles looked at Freddy through the rear view mirror. "My dad raised me the best he knew how. My two older sisters helped out." Charles laughed. "Oh man, did I give them trouble."

Charles turned into the driveway to Eagle's Nest, punched in the security code, and waited until the gates opened wide enough to inch through. "Let's keep our after school arrangement on the Q.T. Your grandmother might not like it."

"I'm not gonna say anything. Uh, I need a favor. Would you pick up a box of Turtles at the Rexall?"

Charles laughed, "You've already got a girlfriend."

.

"If you call a skinny, ugly, despicable teacher, a girlfriend, then I guess you're right."

"Oh, Jesylee Scales, right? She's a legend all right – a petrified one. I guess I can stop by the Rex after I drop your grandmother off at her Jamestowne Society meeting."

Charles drove twice around the circular driveway in front of the estate, tires squealing before pulling under the side portico.

"That was cool," Freddy said. He ambled up the back steps and remembered what Tony had said about the school being haunted. "Oh geez, I hope I don't see any ghosts or spiders." He shivered and a chill went up his spine.

# CHAPTER 11
## CAR STARS

The delicious smell of freshly baked chocolate chip cookies greeted Freddy. He dropped his book bag on the kitchen floor and reached for the cookies still cooling on the countertop.

"I'm starving," Freddy said as he gulped down a whole cookie.

"Freddy Griswold! Shame on you! Where's your manners?" Mrs. McVicker said. "Go wash your hands and then come sit at the table like a proper Wiggie." Mrs. McVicker picked up the backpack and gave Freddy a stern look. "Put this on the hook, sir."

When Freddy returned, Mrs. McVicker had placed a plate of cookies in the center of the table alongside a glass of milk.

Mrs. McVicker leaned back in her chair, "So…how did it go?"

"Oh, it was the greatest day of my life! I only got sent to the principal once."

Mrs. McVicker looked worried. "What on earth did you do?"

"Nothing! Nothing,! Nothing!" Freddy said, his voice booming. "Kids were doing stuff and blaming it on me. A couple of my teachers are real creeps. Miss Scales already hates me." Freddy took his third cookie and a big gulp of milk. "She sent me to the office for no reason. Anyway she hates this guy Tony, too." Mrs. McVicker poured Freddy more milk.

Freddy giggled. "Mrs. Mack, there's a real dorky girl who latched on to me and Tony. She's kinda bossy but she tells some pretty funny jokes."

"It sounds like you're already making friends."

Charles entered the kitchen, picked up a cookie from the table and leaned over pressing the intercom button, "Mrs. Webbe, the car is waiting for you out front." Charles grabbed a couple more cookies. "I'm taking your Grandmother to her Jamestowne Society meeting." Winking at Freddy he said, "I'll pick up a box of Turtles while I'm out."

Dinner was at 5:30. Mrs. McVicker served a delicious pot roast…Freddy mopped up the gravy on his plate with the light, fluffy yeast rolls she made from scratch.

Patting his stomach, Freddy pushed away from the table. "That was so good. Thanks Mrs. Mack."

Beaming, Mrs. McVicker started clearing the table.

"Do you have homework?"

"Yeah…math and history. I guess I'll do it in the library."

Freddy entered the library and surveyed the floor to ceiling built-in oak bookshelves with books of every type and interest. An oriental rug under a massive mahogany table covered the highly polished oak floor. Elegant carved oak millwork surrounded the eight-foot high pocket doors.

The books in the vast library had been catalogued according to the Dewey decimal system. Once a week a volunteer from the St. Wigbod Historical Society reshelved books and worked on historical society business. Adele Webbe's library included classical as well and historical books, first editions of many noted contemporary writers of the twentieth century, and periodicals dating back to 1898. Many scholars and historical society members used her resources regularly.

Freddy pulled out a heavy leather chair, plopped his book bag on the table and dug inside for his math book and notebook paper. By eight o'clock he was tired and his neck was aching. He put his homework away and trudged up the back stairs to his bedroom.

Sitting on the side of the bed, Freddy kicked off his loafers and peeled off his socks; his feet were itchy. He had just decided to take a shower when there was a pounding on his door. In came Charles beaming like the Cheshire Cat in *Alice in Wonderland*. He handed Freddy the box of Turtles.

"Look what else I discovered while at the Rex," he said, holding up a card-sized package wrapped in cellophane, emblazoned with the words *Car\*Stars*.

"What's this?"

"Only the coolest thing to come down the pike since bubblegum," Charles said. "They're kind of like baseball trading cards only these have the stats and everything about cool cars. Open 'um. Let's see what you got."

Freddy tore the clear covering off the cards and carefully laid all five out on his bed. "Oh my gosh, Charles! Here's a 1951 Nash-Healey. That baby can hit 125 mph and it's only 38 inches high!"

The cards had a colored picture of each car with statistics such as awards, speed, engine type, horsepower, and the latest innovations. Freddy held a Hudson Hornet card (145 bhp, 308 cid six) featuring stockcar racer Marshall Teague after a win in his Fabulous Hudson Hornet. Other cards included a 1954 Lincoln Capri V-8 with Hydromantic, a 1955 Chevrolet Bel Air Sport Coupe, and a 1956 Ford Sunliner convertible.

"This is just too cool. Can I get more?"

"That's what fun about them. You trade with your friends. Trade, collect. There's points for speed, design and other stuff. I'd really like to get a 1953 Corvette. Anyway take 'um to school tomorrow and I bet you'll be the envy of every Wiggie in the place," Charles said.

The next morning, armed with a box of Turtles and his cache of *Car*Stars*, Freddy arrived at school. Tony was standing alone under Brave Tree, the school's one hundred year old oak tree, its heavy sprawling bottom limbs propped up by wooden supports.

Freddy raced over to his buddy. "Tony, look at these bad boys!"

"Where did you get 'um?" Tony's exuberance for the *Car*Stars* caught the attention of nearby students. By first bell, dozens of young car enthusiasts were clamoring to see them. By lunch time the word had spread and Wiggies were approaching Freddy in hopes of getting a look at the prized cards.

The second day at Wiggins Prep was turning out to be pretty terrific. By the time sixth period English rolled around, Freddy was prepared to present the chocolate Turtles to Miss Scales and assume a humble demeanor. He held his breath when she accepted his offering. She smiled smugly and told him to return to the back of the room. Freddy stared at her in disbelief.

"But I thought…."

Her crooked smile remained stoic. "We all have our dues to pay." Miss Scales turned her attention to the next student.

Remembering Mr. Hister's warning, Freddy moved to the back of the class. His entire being stung with bitterness. His chest heaved and for the first time in his life he felt the gall of hatred. Freddy watched Miss Scales perform her duties and visualized putting laxative in her Turtles or stealing her lesson plans.

It was hot and stuffy in the classroom even with the windows open; the back of the room was worse. Sweat beaded on Freddy's forehead and he felt queasy. *What's with this crazy old lady? I wish Mama would get well and get me out of here. She always told me to bloom where I'm planted and that nothing is forever.*

Freddy put his head on the desk and closed his eyes. He remembered how he felt when Carly got close to him in Science. Daydreaming, Freddy imagined talking to her.

Startled out of his reverie, a spitball hit the side of his face. Eddie Brinto was holding a straw. "Cut it out!" Freddy mouthed.

Eddie smirked and put his head down.

Students took notes on helping and linking verbs: am, are, is, was, were, be, being, been……. "Memorize

.

these verbs and be ready to recite tomorrow," Miss Scales announced.

With five minutes left in the day, Miss Scales opened her closet door at the front of the classroom. On the side of the closet door hung a mirror and her black veiled pill-box hat. Her traditional end-of-school ritual began. She selected a lipstick, peered into the mirror and carefully colored her lips blood-red. The right side of her face sagged slightly and her top lip drooped. Her hand trembled as she applied the lipstick and the color smeared to her chin. She swiped it clean, pinched her cheeks for color, and powdered her nose. With three hat pins, she secured her hat, pulling the veil over her eyes, and rechecked herself in the mirror. She smiled, retrieved her purse from the middle shelf, closed the closet door and wheeled around to confront the quiet but anguished pupils ready to explode out of the room.

"Remember your assignment for tonight. Think of an event from the beginning of American history that you would like to research. You will decide on a topic, write a thesis sentence, three main ideas with at least four details for each main idea." She gazed into space. "Mr. Gore and I have decided to try a new teaching method. English and history will be integrated. Mr. Gore will take you to the library for your research and I will be supervising the writing, checking grammar, sentence structure, spelling and originality of presentation.  Mr. Gore will grade you on the historical accuracy of your research and knowledge of the subject.  Have your outline ready for review by class time tomorrow."

Her speech was interrupted by the end of school bell.  Her *pets* in row one filed out— Carly Archer, John Stevenson, Kendall Waller, and Anne Dixon.

Next were the "not quite good enough" people: Tony Houlgrave, Molly Martin, Erin Frith and Robert Ford.  The students in row three might as well have not been there.  Miss Scales neither called on them nor looked their way except to give them a chilling nonverbal reprimand; Eustace Clovill, Roger Cooke and Edgar Harrington were used to it.

Today the 'cell block' as she referred to the back of the room was occupied by Freddy and Eddie Brinto.  As Eddie shuffled past, Miss Scales muttered, "Imbecile."

Tony was waiting for Freddy in the hall.  "Hey, man, wanna see the map I got?  It's really cool."

"What's it of?" Freddy asked heading for the exit.

"It's of the lowest basement here.  Wooooo", Tony said waving the map up and down.  "Hardly anyone has ever been down there, 'cept the janitors.  I heard they're even scared...too many weird things have happened—weird noises, ghosts. It's supposed to be real creepy."

Tony was hurrying to keep up with Freddy, "I wanna go down there. You interested?"

"Uh, I don't know." Freddy remembered a scary comic book he'd read about zombies that had scared him so much that he couldn't sleep all night. "How'd we get down there anyway?"

"That's the cool part. My brother Jesse and his friend Dusak are in a car club. To get in the club, you have to go in the lower basement and stay for three minutes. Then you get to be in the 'Chukkas.' They do stuff like go to the races, work on Duzak's rod and other junk."

"I don't know. It does sound kinda interesting, though...going to the races. But the problem is I've got this thing about basements. They scare me. I was locked up in a basement once. I don't know if I can do it."

## CHAPTER 12
## RESEARCH REPORT

C harles was waiting on River Street two blocks from school. Freddy got into the front, threw his book bag into the backseat, and settled into the cushioned comfort of Grandmother Webbe's luxurious car.

"I've got sooo much homework," Freddy groaned. "Miss Scales and Mr. Gore have teamed up...I think they're more than just 'friends'. I see them ogling each other out in the hall."

Freddy stuck his finger down his throat in a gagging gesture. "Can you imagine? Mrs. Scales Gore? YUCK!"

Freddy pulled out one of his *Car\*Stars*, reading the stats on the back. "This says the '53 Lincoln Capri won the first four races in the grueling Mexican Road Race from Tuxtla to Juarez. And check this out...it came in almost an hour in front of a Ferrari. Can you believe it?"

"I did not know that," Charles said, shaking his head in disbelief. "Way to go Capri! So how did the cards go over?"

Freddy said, "Everybody was coming up wanting to see them and wanting to know where to get some. It was super. I bet there'll be lots of trading going on tomorrow." Freddy carefully arranged his cards in a stack and put them in his coat pocket.

"The only thing is they almost got taken away by Mr. Profit. He said he did not want to see 'playthings' out and if he did, they were his. So I've got to be careful."

"Anyhow," Freddy continued, " I've got a full-blown report for homework. Mr. Gore and Miss Scales are working together to torture us."

Charles slowed down to turn onto the lane leading to Eagles' Nest. "Well, you're lucky to have a full-blown library at your disposal."

The massive wrought iron gate emblazoned with an enormous gold W slowly opened. Charles pulled up under the side portico; Freddy grabbed his book bag, ambled up to the backdoor and into the house.

For the second night in a row Freddy found himself in the library at Eagle's Nest, gazing at the imposing library of books. He felt overwhelmed. Seated at the enormous table, Freddy pulled out notebook paper and began to draw. Soon he had sketched an entire battle scene complete with a woman swinging from the gallows. An arrow pointed to the woman. *Scales* was scribbled on the arrow. Exhausted, he put his head down and closed his eyes. His thoughts turned to Miss Scales and seeking revenge. *Her beloved Edgar Allan Poe bust might accidently fall off his pedestal and break into a thousand pieces.* Freddy felt guilty pleasure thinking of the hurt she would feel.

Tiptoeing in, Mrs. McVicker placed a plate of cookies near Freddy. "You need to work on your report, Freddy dear."

Freddy jerked his head up. "I know what I have to do," he snapped.

Mrs. McVicker pulled out a chair near Freddy.

"What's the matter, dear?"

Freddy sat in silence for a moment. "Mrs. McVicker, this stupid school is detestable and full of snotty kids. I don't want to go back. Mama would never put me in such a hideous place."

Mrs. McVicker took Freddy's hand. "I know. Life isn't always fair. But sometimes it can make you stronger." Mrs. McVicker sighed, "Your grandmother is a good example."

"I don't see how. She's rich and can do anything she wants."

Mrs. McVicker handed Freddy a cookie. "Oh, she's had her heartaches, all right. That's why she keeps herself so busy. I'm going to tell you something that few people know. But this is just between you and me."

Freddy stopped chewing.

"Your grandmother lost two babies. Her first was a boy…born several years before your mother. He only lived a few hours. Blue baby they said. Anyway, your grandfather, Dr. Webbe blamed her. That's when she got so involved with the Jamestowne Society."

"Why would he blame Grandmother?" Freddy said.

"That's a mystery. Your Grandmother used to go up to the very room you are staying in and be there for hours. Sometimes I could hear her crying. After a while things seemed to get back to normal."

Freddy reached for a cookie. "What about the other baby?"

"Well, we all got so excited when Mrs. Webbe told us she was expecting again…twins. Dr Webbe seemed to come alive, too. It was a hard pregnancy. She had all kinds of complications. Your mama was born first…but it took hours. By the time her little brother came he was stillborn."

Tears were filling Freddy's eyes. "Oh, poor Grandmother Webbe. I guess you never get over losing a child. Maybe that's why she acts like she does." He thought a moment. "What about my grandfather?"

Mrs. McVicker wiped her eyes with her apron, "He left…never came back.  As far as I know no one has ever seen or heard from him since. Well, enough about that. What about your research report?"

Freddy shrugged.  "I have no idea.  There's too much stuff in here."

Mrs. McVicker wandered over to a section labeled 1600's.  "This is the area about Jamestowne that your grandmother uses. You might start here."  She pulled out a book and handed it to Freddy.

"I don't know.  She probably wouldn't want me handling her Jamestowne books."

"Really, I don't think she'll mind."  Mrs. McVicker picked up the empty cookie plate and left the room.

Freddy opened the book and was impressed with the hand drawings of Indians and their villages. He jotted down notes and finally thought he was ready to make his outline.

The thesis sentence:  Jamestowne, the first English colony established in America had a perilous beginning. Next he must decide on three main ideas.  The book Freddy found most useful was a diary of Sir Thomas Smith, Treasurer of the Council that set out from England on December 19, 1606, to discover new land and riches for themselves and those financing this enterprise.  As Freddy read, the more interesting the topic became.  Soon he was

117

discovering the discontent of those on the three ships heading toward the unknown. The weather was stormy; the crew was insolent and provocative with cries of mutiny. More shocking, was the danger of extinction for the ship's 104 men and boys as they landed at the desired port.

Freddy set to work to complete his outline:

Topic: The Jamestowne Colony

Thesis sentence: Jamestowne, the first English colony established in the new world, had a perilous beginning.

Topic sentence: Sailing across the ocean in 1606 was dangerous, and conditions were treacherous.

Detail: Stormy weather

Detail: Mr. Hunt, the preacher, became seasick and weak

Detail: Crew became discontent with living conditions

Detail: Capt. John Smith was put in chains for insubordination

Topic Sentence: The site selected to begin the first colony was a bad choice.

Detail: Jamestowne was 40 miles up the James River

Detail: Land was low and marshy—little dry land

Detail: the land belonged to the Paspahegh Indians,
    called the Powhatan

Topic sentence: The conditions that the men faced in the
first year were life threatening.

    Detail: Mosquitoes brought disease

    Detail: Attacks by Indians

    Detail: Water polluted—men got sick with dysentery
        and typhoid fever

    Detail: two/thirds of men died the first year

Freddy set back in his chair looking at all the information he had gathered. *I wonder if I had ancestors who lived back then?*

Mrs. McVicker entered the library *clickity clack* on the hardwood floors. "Freddy, you have a telephone call...I didn't get his name—he was whispering."

Freddy placed his outline in his folder and then into his book bag. He followed Mrs. McVicker to the kitchen.

Freddy recognized Tony's voice as soon as he said hello. "I was just working on that thing for Scales," Freddy said.

"What thing?"...

"The outline about early history...due tomorrow, dodo."

.

"Oh no, I forgot. Anyway…remember what I told you about the deep, lower basement?" asked Tony.

"Uh huh" Memories of the time Freddy spent in the basement at Hollow Creek were revived. He'd forgotten to take the key and locked himself in the basement until his mother got home from work. He disturbed a spider's web and it fell into his hair. It bit him and raised quite a bump on his forehead. Freddy felt a chill just thinking about that terrifying experience.

"Tomorrow night my brother and Duzak are gonna take some guys to the school to do the basement. Wanna go?"

Freddy didn't want to appear afraid. *How am I gonna get Tony to stop talking about this?* He said, "Hey Dude, listen. It all sounds cool but you know I can't get out at night."

"Hey, no *problemo*. I can't either. I just wait until my parents go to bed and then I sneak out the side door. You can sneak out and we'll wait for you at the bottom of the hill," Tony explained.

Freddy cupped the phone's mouthpiece, "Maybe some other time. Let's talk about this at school tomorrow."

"Okay. Chukkas Rule!" Tony chanted.

.

"Is that your new friend, dear?" Mrs. McVicker said standing on tiptoes putting plates away in the cabinet. "Your grandmother will be happy that you're making friends."

"I hope something will make her happy. Guess I'll hit the hay. See you in the morning." Freddy stretched and yawned.

Instead of taking the back stairs to his bedroom, Freddy followed the sound of the TV to the study. Grandmother Webbe was knitting and had her shoes off. Her shoulders were covered by a shawl; her red hair was unpinned and hung to her shoulders. She put her knitting down, gazed intently at the television as the time ticked by for the contestant, Dr. Joyce Brothers, to answer the $64,000 question. By now Mrs. Webbe was on the edge of her chair wringing her hands, when the TV host yelled "YOU'RE RIGHT, FOR $64,000!"

Mrs. Webbe jumped up and clapped her hands. "Ellafair, come here…Quick! She got it right."

Mrs. McVicker brushed past Freddy, "Did she win?"

"Yes! I can't believe she knows so much about boxing…All that money. Whoa!" Mrs. McVicker and Mrs. Webbe watched the television as the streamers and balloons descended on the game show stage.

Mrs. Webbe glanced at Freddy with a look of surprise. "Francis, is there something you wanted?"

"I just wanted to tell you I'm doing my history report on Jamestowne."

"Are you?" Grandmother Webbe stared at Freddy and lowered the sound on the TV and plopped down in her chair. "Come in," she said.

Freddy couldn't tell if his grandmother was pleased or offended.

"I could help you find information about Jamestowne. I also have handwritten diaries by the first settlers."

"That would be very helpful, Gran-dama …I mean Grandmother."

"Oh let's not be so formal. Humm, Gran-dama" she said, tasting the sound of it and trying it on for size.

"I like it. Yes, call me Gran-dama." Looking at her watch Gran-dama said, "It's early. Want to watch some television?"

"Sure," Freddy said as he relaxed into the sofa.

Mrs. Webbe adjusted the volume and put her feet on the hassock.

"Oh, before I forget, Miss Scales called and wants to see me," said Gran-dama.

# CHAPTER 13
# THE RAT ROD

Morning dawned gray and overcast. Freddy pulled back the velvet curtains and gazed out. *It's gonna be cold and dreary.*

Methodically, Freddy went through his morning routine...washed his face, checked for pimples, brushed his teeth and combed his hair. Peering into his closet he selected a crisply ironed shirt and his uniform pants. One loafer was under the bed and the other had mysteriously ended up in the bathroom. Freddy brushed his blazer clean before putting it on. He gathered up his outline on Jamestowne from the yellow Formica table he had named Egor and placed it safely in his book bag. He plucked the Quell Stone off the table and dropped it into his pants' pocket.

Freddy smelled the delicious aroma of bacon as he entered the kitchen. Oddly, Mrs. McVicker was nowhere to be seen. Freddy placed his backpack on the hook in the butler's pantry and heard voices and a *clickity clack* sound. The swinging door into the butler's pantry opened and Mrs. McVicker appeared.

.

"Oh, dear me, the bacon's burning! Have you had your orange juice?" Mrs. McVicker raced over to the stove, picked up a hot pad and slid the skillet off the burner. She leaned against a cabinet and adjusted her hair back under her hairnet.

"Mrs. Mack, is everything okay?" Freddy asked.

"Oh, me! Oh, my. Things are a changin' round here. Be a good boy and finish up your breakfast. Charles will be arriving soon to take you to school. You just won't believe what your grandmother just agreed to. Never thought in a million years…."

Freddy became thoughtful. *What could it be? I bet she's sending me away.*

Mrs. McVicker was pacing as if she were a caged lion. "Get your books, Freddy. Hurry! Mr. Charles doesn't have all morning."

Freddy grabbed his book bag and raced out of the kitchen, through the mudroom. He opened the backdoor and heard, a strange sounding horn. "AOOOGA! AOOOGA!" *What the heck…?*

Charles was sitting in the coolest car Freddy had ever seen. He raced around the car, jumping up and down and asking "What is this?"

Mrs. McVicker was at the backdoor clapping her hands with glee. Charles pulled himself out of the driver's side window and landed on his feet with the ease of a gymnast completing a floor exercise.

"How do you like my rat rod?" Charles said.

Freddy couldn't contain himself. "What's in it? How fast will it go? Will you take me for a ride?"

"Freddy, that's exactly what I'm going to do. This is your new ride to school."

"No way! I can't believe it. Is Grand-dama cool with this?"

"Believe it or not your grandmother has a fondness for cool cars. Her father, your great grandfather, worked on designing cars back in the day and apparently she was quite the speedster about town." Charles was beaming now. "So anyway I talked to her about taking you to school in something more hip than the limo. She thought it over for a day or two and yesterday she told me to bring over my rat rod and put it in the garage. This morning she said we'd try out the idea. Hop in. Let's get you to school."

Charles' rat rod had begun life as a 1941 Willys coupe. During its transformation into a rat rod, two inches had been chopped from the roof, the car had been lowered, and a Chevy big block 427 with a turbo 400 automatic transmission supplied power to the huge rear slicks.

Freddy nervously settled himself in the bomber seat and buckled up. Charles once again slid in through the window, buckled up, and fired up the engine. The feel of horsepower was immediate. A rumbling vibration penetrated Freddy's inner core. Charles put the "rat" in gear. The engine roared, the tires spun, and the car shot forward. The sudden acceleration left Freddy feeling light-headed. At the front gate the rat rod screeched to a stop. "Is this fun or what?" Charles yelled.

"That was so cool!" Freddy said trying to catch his breath.

Mrs. McVicker crossed herself as she watched anxiously from under the portico. A face was briefly seen peering out the window of Mrs. Webbe's study. The curtains parted, then fell back into place. Freddy grabbed his pocket and felt the Quell Stone. He smiled as his heart raced and he took a deep breath.

"Now, that was a burnout!" Charles boasted.

"Can we do it again?" asked Freddy.

Suddenly Charles' demeanor changed. Gripping the steering wheel he cleared his throat and continued in a serious tone. "You know, Freddy, driving a hot car is unbelievably exciting but you always have to think of safety. I'd never do what I just did on the street. You could kill yourself or someone else."

"What good is having a fast car if you can't race it?"

"That's what the drag strip is for. We don't have one here so we have to go all the way over to Fenton."

Freddy's face lit up, "Can I go?"

"Your grandmother may not like the idea… but you never know."

Charles pulled out into traffic and kept to the speed limit all the way to Wiggins.

The sound of raw power was strong even as the rat rod sat idling in front of the school. BA RUMPITY RUMP…BA RUMPITY RUMP.

Heads turned to locate the origin of the noise.

Wiggies converged around the car. Older boys arrived and pushed the younger kids out of the way. Duzak and Jesse were the first to poke their necks into the car.

"Hey, man! Where'd you get this souped up machine?" Duzak asked as he looked over the dials and tachometer on the primered dashboard. "Is this a Chevy? Ford? How fast will it go? How did you get it so low? Did you chop it?"

.

Charles grinned. "This is my own creation, son. It's a rat rod and it's faster than anything you'll ever drive."

"Duzak, look it's got an automatic transmission. I bet I could beat it in my grandmother's Conestoga." Jesse said.

Charles just smiled.

"I bet my Merc could blow your doors off," Duzak said.

"You are dreamin', son," Charles said.

"I'm running at Fenton this Friday. Show up and we'll see who's hot and who's not." Duzak said.

Charles laughed at Duzak's boast. "We might see you there." He gave Freddy a knowing look. "Just don't bet anything you can't afford to lose."

# CHAPTER 14
## LOCKED UP

Life began to take on a sense of routine for Freddy. However, he felt his life was in limbo because he still had not seen his mother. His grandmother kept promising to take him to see her but then made excuses and said they would go another day. Freddy was getting more and more frustrated. He considered asking Tony's brother, Jesse, to take him to the hospital.

Charles took Freddy to school and picked him up in his rat rod. Now Freddy wanted Charles to pick him up at the front of the school. Freddy tried out for the choir and made it. Rehearsals were after school from 4:00 – 5:30 on Tuesdays and Thursdays. After choir rehearsal on Tuesdays, Freddy and Tony stayed for piano lessons until 7:00 in the evening.

After piano Charles usually picked up Freddy but occasionally Tony's sixteen-year-old brother, Jesse took Freddy home whenever Charles had to drive Mrs. Webbe to a Jamestowne Society meeting.

It was at such a time when Freddy and Tony found themselves waiting for a ride after their piano lessons on that uncommonly cold October evening. Mr. Flowers had to leave promptly at seven o'clock to make it to the St. Wigbod Symphony rehearsal by 7:30. He left the two boys practicing their boogie-woogie piano duet they planned to perform at the Thanksgiving Musical. Tony checked his new Timex military style wristwatch he had received for his birthday.

"Holy moly!  We gotta s-s-plit," Tony shouted. "It's 7:15. Duzak will have a c-c-cow."

"Get going! I'll catch up," Freddy said, stuffing his music into his book bag. He caught up with Tony on the stairs to the front entrance. The security gate was locked. Tony shook the heavy metal gate but it would not budge.

"We're locked in," Freddy said, his heart pounding.

"There's a side door on the lower level that's usually open. The janitors use it. Let's check it."

They raced down the marble stairs, their footsteps echoing in the empty corridor until they reached the lower level. It was shadowy and dimly lit; concrete had replaced the highly polished marble floors from above. "Do you know where we are?"  Freddy whispered.

"I've only been down here once." Tony pointed to the right. "I think it's down this way".  They proceeded with barely an inch between them. Overhead the pipes huffed and heaved and hissed alive with steam. A shadowy figure was moving towards them. Tony stopped in his tracks and Freddy ran into him. They stumbled tried to regain balance but went down on the cold floor.

"HEY! What are you doing down here?" barked the approaching figure.

"We got locked in. Mr. Flowers had to leave and…and Tony said we could get out this way," Freddy blathered, looking up and breathing fast.

"Who said you could come down here?"

Tony and Freddy were still on the floor. "M-m-my brother brought me out this way once."

"Who's your brother?"

"Jesse Houlgrave,"

"Oh, so you're Jesse's little Wiggie brother, hey?" The man had a beard and was dressed in a blue Dickies' shirt and pants. He reached down and pulled Tony to his feet.

Freddy stood dusting himself off.

"So—you got names?"

"I'm Tony and he's Freddy…first year…doesn't know his way around."

"Doesn't look like you do either…First off, you shoulda gone left. That's where I live down yonder," he said pointing to the end of the hall. "Name's Bartholomew Gosnoll. My great, great, grandfather was one of the original 104 that came to America on *The Susan Constant*— great little ship. Founded Jamestowne, they did." Mr. Gosnoll's chest expanded with pride. "Yeah, couldn't even work here if I didn't have connections to Jamestowne. Anyhows, everyone calls me Bart. You know the names of the other ships that landed at Jamestowne?"

"How would anybody know that?" Tony said.

"I do…I do!" Freddy said. "I'm doing my research paper on Jamestowne. There were three ships in all…The Susan Constant, Godspeed and Discovery."

"Right you are," Bart said and reached for Freddy's hand with his own calloused one and pumped it up and down. Bart motioned for the two boys to follow him. "Shhhhh…don't want to wake up the ghosts." Bart stepped lightly, tip-toeing and raising his legs in an exaggerated movement. Freddy and Tony followed close behind. A mouse scampered under a pile of debris. Cobwebs hanging on gossamer threads clung to their hair.

"Are we safe?" Freddy whispered.

Bart wheeled around, grabbed Freddy by the neck and shoulders and yelled, "BOO!"

Freddy felt his legs go weak, his heart skipped a beat. This was scarier than facing Mr. Hister.

"HA! HA! HA! HA!" Bart roared. "I bet you little Wiggies peed your pants!"

"That wasn't funny," Freddy said.

"Come on now you little fraidy cats. I was only funnin'."

"Well, I'm not laughing," Freddy shot back.

At last they reached the end of the dank smelling hall and the battered screen door leading outside. Freddy cautiously opened the gritty door, looked to his left and saw a weathered door, its green paint chipped. A foggy mist was seeping out from beneath the rotted door jamb. On the wall above the door a gooey substance was oozing out as though the wall was bleeding.

"Where's that door go to?" Freddy said motioning to the mist.

"Oh, now that leads down to the lowest levels of the lower basement where the ghosties live, don't you know." He lowered his voice. "Parts of it I don't go myself. They who goes down there comes back crazy-like." Bart circled his finger around his temple and rolled his eyes.

Freddy and Tony bounded up the cracked concrete steps to the sidewalk on Tidewater Street. Running, slipping and sliding, they skidded around the corner and reached the front of the school.

In front was *The Merc*, Duzak's 1949 metallic purple Mercury. Out of breath, palms clammy, Tony frantically tried to open the car door but the handle kept slipping out of his fingers.

"Hey little brother. What's the matter? You're acting like you just seen a ghost," Jesse said rolling down the window.

"Jesse, open the door," screamed Tony.

Jesse's attempt to open the car door was hampered by Tony and Freddy scrambling over each other to get in the backseat.

"Hey, droolies, watch what you're doin," Duzak ordered. "Don't put your feet on the seats. I just finished doin' the upholstery. Where you jugheads been anyway? We been waitin' out here in the cold for fifteen minutes."

"The front gate was locked and so we went down to the b-b-basement to try and get out," Tony said, wheezing. "Old B-B-Bart nearly scared the bo didley out of us with his h-h-h-ollarin' and yelling about ghosts."

"Hey, Bart's a good guy. Maybe not the sharpest tool in the shed...but he lets us use the lower basement for our *Chukka* initiations. Hey, Tony said you want to get in the club. That right, Fredaroni?" Duzak turned the ignition on and *The Merc* came to life.  He burned rubber around the circular drive.

Duzak was the kind of guy that everyone thought was cool.  He had an indefinable quality.  His hair was thick and wavy; girls loved to run their fingers through his dark tresses.  He walked with a bit of a swagger but he was not cocky.  His blue eyes radiated and illuminated warmth.  He always looked neat and preppy at school but on weekends he transformed himself into a hot rod king.  The Chukkas gathered at Duzak's house to work on cars and hang out.  His smile was electric and his heart pure gold.  Still, he had failed two times while in elementary school.  Now he was sixteen, the oldest in his ninth grade class, and the only one who owned a car and had a driver's license.

Freddy felt anxious about Duzak taking him home.  "Uh, my grandmother's expecting Jesse to be driving me home in his grandmother's car.  If she sees me in *The Merc* she'll never let anyone give me a ride home again."

Duzak downshifted.  "No worries. We ditched the 'lead sled' about three blocks from your house.  First we're gonna make a pass by the Oasis and check out the Wiggettes." He winked at Jesse.  "Then we'll get you home before bed check.  A little advice to the wise…sweaty palms are a real turnoff for girls.  I'd leave those at home if I were you."

A block from the Oasis Drive-In, Duzak eased over to the curb, and combed his wavy hair into a ducktail. Jesse was busy arranging his greasy pompadour back into shape. Both boys were wearing white t-shirts, black leather jackets, blue jeans, and their coveted brown suede Chukka boots.

Duzak circled the OA and gunned the motor a few times. "No action tonight. This place is dead."

Jesse said, "Whadja expect? It's bad luck to bring a couple of uninitiated Chukkas to cruise the OA." He turned in his seat and punched Tony on the shoulder with his fist, "Just kiddin' little bro."

Duzak brought *The Merc* to a complete stop. He revved the motor a couple of times and peeled out, smoking the tires. "Okay let's get goin' before Heckle and Jeckle back there turn into pumpkins."

"Better not peel outta here," Jesse said. "The cops are waiting for you."

******

Jesse's grandmother's Studebaker Conestoga station wagon was parked in front of the Green Frog Lounge; the lounge sign flashed on and off as a big green frog tipped his top hat on and off his head.

Jesse got out of *The Merc* and slid into the driver's side of the Conestoga. Tony claimed shotgun and Freddy climbed into the backseat. Duzak put *The Merc* in first and speed shifted down King James Street burning rubber all the way.

A police car, lights flashing and siren on, whizzed by. "Uh, oh! Duzak's getting' a ticket," Jesse said. "It'd be his second this month...guess he won't be driving for a while."

Another police car passed followed by two fire engines.

"What's going on? They can't all be after Duzak," Freddy said.

Jesse said, "Somethin' big's happening. Let's follow um."

Freddy's adrenalin kicked in. "Hey, I see smoke in South Town but, we'd better not go across the tracks. I've heard white kids need to stay out of that part of town."

Jesse got the wagon on the road, following other cars going in the direction of the fire trucks. He said, "What can happen? We won't stay long."

When they crossed the tracks into South Town the appearance of the neighborhood changed. The streets were narrow with chuckholes, and row tenement buildings came up to the sidewalks. People were gathered around fifty-five gallon drums, burning wood, cardboard, tires... anything that could burn and keep them warm. Women carrying babies, men in flannel shirts and older kids were running in the same direction.

Jesse parked and the three joined the crowd moving toward the sirens and flashing lights. At the intersection Freddy saw the sign: Hallelujah Baptist Church. A white cross was burning in the yard; windows in the sanctuary were broken. Firemen worked to extinguish the flames as the charred cross smoked. A man holding a Bible was speaking. "Do not let the evil doers or the haters win. We will stand tall and fight this with our faith. Take that first step even when you can't see the whole staircase. Truth and love will have the final word."

Freddy recognized the man— Mr. Boangeres, Bo. Freddy ran up to him. "Do you remember me? You gave me a ride a while back."

"Sho do! It's Freddy, right?"

"What happened here?" Freddy looked around at the sadness of the scene.

Bo said, "The Klan."

"What's that?

"Oh son, there's people has so much hate in their heart. They hate us for the color of our skin, jus' 'cause we're alive. These people are really cowards. They hide themselves under white robes and white pointy hats while they destroy our houses, churches and businesses."

"But why?"

Bo looked at Freddy, his eyes welling up, "It's jus' the way things is right now. But we's strong people and in time all Gods' people will be equal."

"Is there anything I can do to help?"

"Yes they is. Jus' love yo fellow man and try yo best to stamp out injustice where ever you sees it. Well, you'd best be goin'. No tellin' what might happen next. You better stay clear of this side of town 'cause lots of brothers don't take to white folk."

Freddy didn't understand but he sensed he should do as Bo suggested. As the guys walked back to the car, Freddy turned to see Bo preaching, the charred cross his backdrop. Freddy couldn't quite put his finger on it but deep down inside he felt guilty and ashamed.

******

The Conestoga pulled into the driveway at Eagle's Nest at 8:30 p.m. Freddy was not looking forward to explaining to Gran-dama why he was so late getting home from piano lessons.

"Punch in 1956 on the keypad," Freddy said. "Hurry! I just hope Gran-dama's asleep or something."

Jesse punched the numbers but the gate wouldn't open. He tried again. Nothing happened. "It's too dark. I can't see."

Freddy slid across the back seat, rolled down the window, stretched to reach the keypad and entered the code. The heavy gate began to open and Jesse screeched the tires as he accelerated up the drive.

"I don't believe it. The limo's not here," Freddy said, relieved. "We either have just lucked out big time or I'm in sooo much trouble."

Freddy turned to see car lights turning onto the lane. "Quick! Out of the car." '.

The three boys huddled together on the porch; Freddy rang the bell. "Mrs. Mack! Open up!"

The outside porch light came on. "Just a minute, Freddy dear. Let me find the right key. Be right back."

Freddy screamed in panic, "Mrs. Mack, there's a spare key above the doorsill. Hurry!"

"Oh goodness me. I forgot about that. There it is." Mrs. Mack unlocked the door, the boys rushed in, jabbering all at once and each slid to a chair at the kitchen table.

"We sure would like some of your delicious cookies…and milk," Freddy said with a nervous smile.

Mrs. McVicker looked at the boys. "You certainly are in a rush. You haven't been into mischief, have you?" She got a plate from the cabinet and counted out twelve cookies from the cookie jar and placed them on the table.

The mudroom door opened. Freddy heard the sound of chatter and Mrs. Webbe brushing off her shoes. Freddy heard Charles say something about young people using their imaginations to create better ideas. Then his grandmother said, "Right you are, Charles. Papa took me out to the dry lake once in his Duesenberg and opened her up full throttle. He said we hit 116 mph. What an absolute thrill! Think your rat rod could beat that?" Mrs. Webbe laughed.

"I don't know but I'm pretty sure I could beat Duzak's Merc," Charlie replied.

Grandmother Webbe entered the kitchen, looked at her watch and then at the boys eating cookies and drinking milk. Why are you having a cookie party at this hour? Jesse, you need to get Freddy home by 7:30."

Jesse said, "I'm so sorry about the time, Mrs. Webbe, but I had to stop for gas and then my brother asked me to take him to the library. Anytime you have something to do I'll be glad to give Francis a ride home and I'll be sure to get him back on time." Jesse finished his milk and took a hasty exit.

.

Mrs. Webbe picked up a cookie. "Did you see that smoke in South Town? I wonder what that was all about?"

# CHAPTER 15
## THE FINAL VISIT

Saturdays were special for Freddy. He woke up late, lounged in bed or studied his *Car\*Stars* which had grown to fifty-eight cards. Some cars had bonus points for looks, horsepower, top speed, which added to the overall desirability of ownership. This morning, Freddy was admiring one of his high pointers.

There was a soft knock at his door. The door opened and a head peeked around.

Freddy jumped up surprised, "Gran-dama! Did I do something?"

"No, no. I just wanted to chat."

"Come in." He directed her to the yellow chrome chair. "Have a seat."

Grandama looked at the yellow tape covering the tears on the plastic. "Oh, horrors! This tacky thing should be thrown out."

"It's okay," Freddy said, "I call the table Egor."

Gran-dama sat down at the Formica table while Freddy perched on the edge of his bed. Mrs. Webbe looked around the room shaking her head. She got out the handkerchief she carried in the sleeve of her housedress and began polishing the chrome around the table. "This room is just hideous. Look at those drapes. This is no place for a boy."

Freddy didn't know what to do or say so he smiled and shrugged his shoulders.

"Well anyway...I wanted to talk to you about your mother. I have been visiting her and getting reports about her progress from her doctor. Up until yesterday she has been in a deep coma. Her doctor didn't want you to see her before now because of her fragile condition."

Freddy's eyes widened. "Did she wake up?"

"She's been coming in and out of conscientiousness— she asked for you."

Freddy jumped up, his *Car*Stars* scattering, "When can I see her?"

"Today...this morning...after you get some breakfast."

Freddy was already out of his pajamas pulling on his jeans. "Oh thank you. I'm ready. I'll just get some orange juice."

"Don't forget your shoes." Mrs. Webbe took another look at Freddy's room when she noticed the knick-knack shelf. She walked to the shelf and picked up an angel."Your mother collected angels when she was little. She said they protected her.  It might be nice if you took her one."

Mrs. Webbe gazed at Freddy.  "Come get me when Charles comes around with the car."

The ride to the county hospital took an hour. Although Charles had the radio turned down low, Freddy could still hear the sounds of *The Great Pretender* by the Platters, *Que Sera Sera* by Doris Day and *Wonderful, Wonderful* by Johnny Mathis.  Freddy heard Gran-dama humming along while she knitted. He stared out the window. The trees were bare and the grass brown.  A northern wind had blown in making the world seem cold and hostile.  Then the DJ announced, "Let's step it up a notch and get our blood pumping…here's Elvis Presley and Heartbreak Hotel."

Freddy's grandmother covered her ears. "Charles, turn that racket off.  Why they let such awful stuff go out over the air waves I'll never know."

The sign for Bruster County Hospital appeared. Charles turned onto the tree lined boulevard leading to the hospital.  The imposing white façade appeared sterile and unfriendly.  A few people were bracing the wind, running to get out of the cold.  Charles rolled to a stop at the loading area.  He held the door open for Mrs. Webbe and Freddy with one hand as his other hand held on to his hat. They scooted out of the back seat, the wind pounding against them.   With their heads down they braced themselves against stinging pea size gravel and tiny hailstones that pelted them as they pushed against the wind and struggled to open the large hospital doors.

Two orderlies rushed to help, putting their shoulders against the unwieldy entrance doors.   Gran-dama and Freddy literally blew in. "I have never seen such a force." Mrs. Webbe said.  "It's an ill wind that blows no good."

Mrs. Webbe saw her reflection in the mirror across from where they stood, and patted down her hair. "Come, Francis. Let's go see your mother."

Freddy followed his grandmother to the fourth floor. They stopped at room 425. Mrs. Webbe took Freddy by the hand and looked him in the eyes. "Don't be alarmed. She's hooked up to hoses and machines to help her breathe. She wants to see you." Mrs. Webbe squeezed Freddy's hand and opened the door.

Freddy was startled by the paraphernalia connected to his mother but he stifled a gasp. Walking to the side of his mother's bed, Freddy bent down and kissed her on the forehead. Hannah's eyelids fluttered and opened slightly. "Freddy?"

.

"Yes Mama. How are you doing?

Her voice was frail, a whisper. "Been better." She managed a faint smile and reached for Freddy's hand. Mouthing the words, she said softly, "How's school?"

Freddy sat on the side of the bed. "Pretty good...I like it...When do you think you'll come home?"

"Soon." Hannah closed her eyes.

Freddy softly rubbed his mother's arm.

Her breathing became regular and deep. Freddy looked at his Grandmother. "I think she's asleep. Grandama, would you like to hold Mama's hand?"

Mrs. Webbe nodded and changed places with Freddy. Freddy was holding onto the angel he had brought and put it in his mother's hand. Mrs. Webbe stroked her daughter's face. "So much needless time has gone by. Oh, if only we could change the past."

Hannah's eyes opened slightly and she incoherently uttered, "Drifted off." She shifted her position and noticed the angel in her hand. She breathed, "Lacy. Watch me." Hannah put Lacy at her side. "Mama...thank you....Freddy... handful."

"Don't you worry. Charles is teaching Francis all about cars and he's making nice friends." Mrs. Webbe went to the window and peered out at the blustery day. "Your job is to get well." She glanced at her watch. "But we'd better go. The doctor told us not to stay too long." Mrs. Webbe returned to Hannah's bedside. "I love you. Please forgive me."

Drifting back to sleep, Hannah sighed. "Love… you… forgiven."

Mrs. Webbe gazed at Hannah, her eyes welling, as though it was the last time she would see her daughter.

"Can I call you?" Freddy said to his mother.

Mrs. Webbe said, "There's no phone in the room. We'll come back tomorrow."

Freddy said, "I love you, Mama. See you soon."

Mrs. Webbe led the way to the door. Freddy turned. He hurried back to his mother. "Get better Mama. We need you. I love you and think about you every day." Her eyes were closed. He blew her a kiss.

The next day, Freddy woke to learn his mother had died peacefully.

******

Nothing could have prepared Freddy for the grief and utter desolation he was feeling. After the funeral amenities were over, and every guest had left Eagle's Nest, the house became a tomb of silence. Grandama climbed the stairs to her bedroom and locked the door. Mrs. McVicker left a tray of food outside Mrs. Webbe's room three times a day.

Freddy longed for his mother and cried alone in his room until he could cry no more. Mrs. McVicker tried to console Freddy. She made his favorite dishes and baked him delicious cookies. One evening Freddy was in the kitchen. Mrs. McVicker offered him some freshly baked cookies.

Freddy snapped at her, "I'm not hungry. Leave me alone."

Mrs. McVicker looked shaken and said, "Freddy, when you are ready to talk, I'll be here to listen."

Freddy turned and ran back up to his room. He thought he would never feel happy again. Misery and sadness were his constant companions. He didn't want to live without his best friend, his mother. His thoughts turned dark with depression. Freddy began to think that death would be a comfort over the pain and suffering he was enduring. Thoughts of ending his life tormented and beckoned him. Thinking back to his science class he remembered that apple seeds are poisonous and if he ate enough they could poison him.

That evening Freddy slipped into the kitchen and gathered six apples and grabbed a knife. He returned to his room and placed the apples and the knife on Egor. Purposefully Freddy began slicing the apples and removing the seeds. A vision of his mother appeared holding out her hands and mouthing "Don't! Don't! Don't!"

As if awakened from a trance, Freddy realized what he was planning. Thoughts raced though his mind. *Live for your mother...choose life.* In that moment Freddy's head cleared and he vowed to never let death tempt him again. He knew he must live for himself and his mother.

Freddy cut the apples into small pieces, wrapped them in toilet tissue and threw them in the trash.

# CHAPTER 16
## SURPRISE VISITOR

It was four days after his mother's death, five days before Thanksgiving and two days before the Thanksgiving Musical. Duzak stood in the foyer of Eagle's Nest, hands in his pockets, studying the painting named *The Battle of Waterloo*.

"Hey, Duzak. What's goin' on?" Freddy said, greeting him in the foyer.

"Cool painting. Is it real?" Duzak was surveying the devastated French army in the scene by Mark Churms.

"Yeah, I guess." The pair stared at the painting for a few more seconds.

"We haven't seen you too much lately. Sorry about your mom. The guys were wondering how you're doing?"

Freddy looked at the floor. "Okay. I guess."

"Well, the Chukkas and me were wondering if you might want to go for a Coke? We're gonna meet at the Rex... You know, play the juke and stuff."

Freddy shrugged. "Maybe. I don't know if I could get out though. My grandmother's still staying in her room. Hasn't been down since…you know. Maybe Charles could drop me off."

"Okay. We just thought you might like to get out…So maybe we'll catch you later," Duzak said. Freddy walked Duzak to the front door, its stained glass panels glistening. As he stepped onto the porch, Duzak gave Freddy a nod and a thumbs up, sprinted over to *The Merc*, and slowly drove away.

Freddy wondered if Carly would be at the Rexall. Maybe he should go out. He looked for Charles and found him in the garage setting the timing on his hot rod. "Hey, Charles. Uh… A friend of mine just stopped by."

"That's good." Charles' arm reached back, "Hand me that five-eighths socket on the table."

Freddy put the socket in Charles' hand. "Anyway, he said the kids are meeting at the Rex. Do you think you could give me a lift over there? It'd probably only be for just an hour or two."

Charles wiped his hands on a red rag. "I don't know, Freddy…I don't know how your grandmother would feel."

"She hasn't come out of her bedroom since the funeral. For all she knows I could have run away. She doesn't care about me."

.

"I know, buddy.    It hurts a lot.    But your grandmother is suffering, too.  Tell you what.  I'll drop you off at the Rex but only for about an hour and a half.  I've got to get some plugs for the rat rod and other stuff.  But boy, you have to be ready to leave when I get there to pick you up."

"I promise." Freddy said with sincerity.  "What do you think I should wear?"

"What do the other kids wear?"

"Mostly jeans, I guess, and T-shirts.

"Wait here just a minute. I've got something for you." Charles headed off to his room in the basement.

Freddy ambled over to the rat rod and was looking under the hood at the 427 when Charles trotted back carrying a package. "I was going to wait until Christmas but here's something you could use right now." Charles handed the box to Freddy.  "It's not wrapped, but what the heck."

Freddy took the top off.    Inside was a red windbreaker.

Charles was beaming. "Try it on."

Freddy put the windbreaker on and checked it for fit.

"Well look at you…You look just like James Dean in *Rebel Without a Cause*," Charles said.

Freddy took the jacket off and put it back in the box. Tears began streaming down his face and he fell to the floor heaving great sobs. Charles settled down beside Freddy and hugged him tightly. Freddy burrowed his head into Charles' chest. His sorrowful weeping finally subsided. Freddy wiped his eyes, "Thanks Charles. You're like a father to me."

"That's a great thing for you to say. Do you feel better?"

"A little, maybe. I just miss Mama so much. Will I ever feel good again?"

"It'll take a while. But if your Mama was here she'd tell you to go on living. She wouldn't want you to stay home and feel sorry for yourself."

"I know you're right. I really do want to see my friends. Maybe I should go meet them at the Rex."

******

Charles dropped Freddy off at the Rexall at 8:30 p.m.

"Be out in front at ten o'clock or your name is mud, son."

154

"Don't worry. See you at ten." Freddy felt in his pocket for his Quell Stone, rubbed it and felt calmer. Two sparks whizzed out the seam.

Coming out of the Rexall were some teenagers Freddy didn't recognize. They were laughing, giggling, and singing *Tutti Frutti Oh, Rutti*. Then, they all lined up in front of Freddy…"Tutti frutti, oh, rutti, wop-bop-a-loo mop a- lop-bon-bon, wooo…"

Freddy sauntered into the Rexall and looked around for anyone he knew. There were kids in booths, some at tables, and others gathered around the juke box. Ricky Nelson's *I'm Walking* was playing.

"Fredaroni! Over here!" came a voice through the crowd. Gathered around Duzak at the far end of the counter were Tony, Jesse, Eddie and Eustace—the Chukkas. All five were wearing white t-shirts, sleeves rolled up, (except for Duzak who was wearing a black t-shirt), pegged blue jeans, and their Chukka boots.

"What's up?" Freddy said joining the group.

"Hey, I like the rebel look," Duzak said, rubbing the windbreaker.

"Yeah, I just got it from Charles."

Freddy looked around sizing up the girls. Most were wearing full skirts over lots of petticoats held in by a waist cincher, white bobby socks and either saddle oxfords or penny loafers. In a booth, four girls kept eyeing Freddy and the Chukkas. Two girls scooted out and headed in Freddy's direction. Freddy recognized Carly from school. *Boy, does she look different!* Carly was wearing a white cashmere sweater turned around backwards, buttoned up the back, and a red straight skirt, a bit tight across her hips. Black flats completed her look. As she walked, her hips swiveled in an alluring way and awakened something in Freddy he had never experienced before. Her black shoulder length hair swayed and glistened in the light.

The two girls approached the Chukkas. Carly smiled at Freddy and brushed against him. "Freddy, I'm so sorry. I didn't mean to run into you," she said, her eyes fluttering.

"I was actually in your way." Freddy looked into her eyes and then at the floor.

Carly touched his arm. "I hear you and Tony are playing a rockin' piano duet for the Thanksgiving Musical."

"We're gonna try."

"I'll be in the front row. You'll do great. Oh, I'm so rude. I didn't introduce you to my cousin Cotton. She's from Alabama."

"Nice to meet you. You here for Thanksgiving?" Freddy shook her hand.

"For a whole week. Gobble, gobble." Cotton seemed a little awkward.

Carly grabbed her cousin's hand, "We're on our way to the girl's room. Gotta powder our noses." The two giggled and sashayed away.

Jesse slapped Freddy's back. "Someone's sizzlin'!"

Tony went over to the juke box, put in a nickel and selected *Rock Around the Clock* by Bill Haley. The whole place started jivin'. Carly and Cotton came out of the bathroom swinging and swaying to the music. Halfway through the song Carly approached Freddy. "Are you gonna to ask me to dance or not?"

"I don't know how."

"Who cares?" Carly grabbed his hand pulled him over to the dance floor and started doing a brand-new dance called the twist. Freddy felt a little spastic at first but got the hang of it and by the end of the song he was winded and his knees rubbery. They stood in awkward silence when *All I Have to do is Dream* by the Everly Brothers started playing. Freddy reached for Carly's hand and they began dancing in place. Freddy could smell her perfume, and the aroma of her freshly washed hair. By the end of the song Freddy felt weak with love.

# CHAPTER 17
## CHUKKA INITIATION

F reddy was still feeling the glow when he ambled back to the guys. Duzak put his hand on Freddy's shoulder.

"The guys and me were talkin' and thought that tonight would be a good time to make you a bona fide Chukka. So what do you think? You up for it?"

"I don't know." Freddy looked over at Carly and smiled. *How am I gonna get out of this?* "What do I have to do?"

"Let's decide over a drink. Want a cherry Coke or maybe a cherry phosphate?"

"Uh, just a Coke," Freddy said.

Duzak patted Freddy on the back, "Good choice. Eustace, get us all some Cokes. So anyway, as I was sayin', all you have to do is spend three minutes in the lower basement at the school. Just three measly minutes."

"Where will you guys be?" Freddy checked his watch and felt for the Quell Stone. *How can I say no and*

158

*not look like a total wimp?* His mind was racing for a way out.

"We'll be right there with you, buddy. Ol' Bart's gonna leave the door unlocked until eleven. Tonight's the night. Let's do it." Duzak raised his clinch-fisted arm in the air.

"Oh no, I just remembered," Freddy said, "I can't do it. There's not enough time, cuz...uh...Charles is going to pick me up at ten and it's already past nine. If I'm not out front by ten, my behind is toast."

The soda jerk appeared with six Cokes bubbling, full of chipped ice. Duzak took a sip. "Don't worry, Fredaroni. We've got plenty of time. We'll be back way before ten. Huh, guys?"

Freddy heard, "Oh yeah...Plenty of time...No *problemo*... For the Chukkas!"

"I can't. I'm allergic to scorpions and the place has to be crawling with them." Freddy said.

"Dusak slapped his knee and laughed, "It just so happens that there are no scorpions down there. Bart sprays for them. It's as clean as Mrs. McVicker's floor."

Freddy stared into space and rubbed his Quell Stone. He didn't know what else to say. "Okay, but I REALLY have to be back by ten." Freddy hated being intimidated by these guys.

.

*The Merc* was parked across the street from the Rex. It had been hand washed and dried. Under the full moon the metallic paint and chrome sparkled like cut glass. Freddy, Tony and Eustace shared the backseat. Jesse was riding shotgun and Eddie was squeezed in the middle. Duzak fired up *The Merc*, revved her twice, peeled off, and swerved, just missing a cat.

"Close one," Duzak said

"We don't need any road kill, especially tonight, Dude," Jesse said" His knuckles white from gripping the door handle.

The streets of St. Wigbod were deserted except for the occasional wino propped against a building. *The Merc* screeched to a stop on River Street at 9:17 p.m.

"The Lady" loomed—dark and menacing. "Everybody out. Let's do this thing," Duzak said.

On the sidewalk, Duzak explained the plan. Everyone would go down to the lower basement; Duzak would lead. Eddie would stay out on the sidewalk as lookout. After everyone was gathered in the basement, Jesse would take Freddy to the entrance of the Chukka initiation room. Freddy would go in by himself and stay for three minutes yelling CHUKKAS RULE! When the three minutes were up, Eustace would blow the whistle he had swiped from The Beast and Freddy could come out.

Except for Duzak, the others were huddled, hands in their pockets, shivering. Duzak was animated, excited, "Got the plan, man? Ready? Yo, Eustace, check the door. See if it's unlocked."

"I don't want to. You do it." Eustace said.

"What's the matter? You scared?" Duzak taunted.

"I just don't want to."

"For crying out loud! Jesse, check the door."

"I think *you* should do it," Jesse shot back. "It's your plan."

"My plan, my car…you're acting like a bunch of wimps." Duzak stomped off. He hesitated at the door and looked up at the corner. White ooze bubbled down the wall leaving a vapory mist. He turned the door knob. The door opened and he smelled the stench of death. Duzak covered his nose with the sleeve of his jacket. "Oh puke."

"Yo, Duzak! Everthing all right?" Jesse called.

"Just peachy keen. The door's open. Come on."

As the guys entered, each one gagged. The stench was overwhelming.

"Something just died in here," Eustace said coughing.

"I don't think it's safe to come in here," Freddy said, hoping the whole thing would be called off.

"Frederoni, don't be chicken. Nothing's going to get you," Dusak said, his bravado sounding weak.

Duzak led the way using his Zippo lighter to break the darkness. The creaking stairs were narrow; cobwebs and strings of dust roped like sheaths of cotton candy hitting and covering their shoulders, face, and hair.

Tony was the first to flail his arms striking at the flimsy dust warriors.

"Ahhh, what's touching me?" Tony screeched, grabbing at Duzak almost knocking him off the stairs.

"Cut it out. What're you trying to do, kill me?" Duzak yelled as he reached the basement floor.

Freddy grabbed a wooden post and froze in place.

"Keep moving, man," Eustace said

"You go ahead." Freddy said, strangled with panic.

"Come on. Calm down," Tony reassured Freddy. "Let go of the post and scramble the rest of the way down."

*How'd I let them talk me into this?* Waves of panic gripped him. Freddy stumbled down the creaky stairs and landed in a heap of grime.

A monstrous furnace boiled water that sent steam and heat to all parts of the school. The rumble of the roaring boiler sounded like a bellowing, belching, hungry ogre; its red eyes flashing with fire. The ceiling was low, covered in ash and soot. Piles of ancient, discarded desks, blanketed in dust were stacked and strewn about. Lumber, bricks, and trash littered the floor. Old paint cans were home to rats, centipedes and spiders. Duzak told Jesse to take Freddy to the initiation room.

Freddy inhaled deeply but stood rooted to the floor. His knees were weak; he thought he might faint.

"Tony's already been initiated and he's younger than you. He passed with flying colors," Duzak prodded.

Tony said, "It's not that b-b- bad, Freddy. When it's over, you'll feel proud" Slowly, Freddy began to move." He closed his eyes as Jesse led him to the room.

The air became cold and dank. At the entrance, Freddy felt the breath of a cold spirit. Shivers shot up his spine. He gripped the Quell Stone, hoping it could save him.

Jesse's pupils were dilated and his hands shaking. He whispered to Freddy, "Okay, Buddy, you're on your own. All you gotta do is go into that room and stay for three minutes. Oh yeah, don't forget to yell, 'Chukkas rule' while you're in there." Jesse ran back, out of breath and feeling light-headed.

Freddy's heart was throbbing in his ears. LUB DUB... LUB DUB...LUB DUB. He stepped into the dark cave-like room. He squeezed the Quell Stone tighter. Rubbing it sent a deluge of sparks flying, lighting up the room. Water was dripping…something brushed against his leg and he stepped in something slick. Then, he heard a ghostly sound, "Come Freddy…come. Come Freddy…come." Strobing orange, yellow and red lights vibrated before his eyes. Purple and blue tones swirled and danced in and out, merging with the orange and red. He was dizzy from the blasting color explosion. A gravitational force pulled him toward the blinding lights.

"Come Freddy, come. Come Freddy, come." He resisted but the force pulled until he was swept into its powerful tentacles. He was being sucked through a wormhole into space past brilliant exploding fireworks of shimmering emerald greens and iridescent purple, blue and turquoise force fields. A burst of blinding white light and an ear shattering blast of sound propelled him out and onto the other side.

## CHAPTER 18
## THE SUSAN CONSTANT

A storm was raging. Water pounded Freddy's face. He tried to stand but was struck down by the rocking, rolling tempest.

"Ahoy! Who goes here?" a man said, bracing himself against the wind. "Stand and declare yourself."

Freddy looked at the man in bewilderment. "Where am I?"

"Criminy lad! You're aboard the *Susan Constant.*

"Who are you? Is this part of the initiation?" Freddy said looking over the ship and trying to figure out what had happened.

"You must be dazed. I'm Captain Newport. We're bound for the New World…by the authority of King James I of England." The man of forty-seven was dressed in puffy brown leather shorts, white stockings, and black knee-high boots. His form-fitting, bedazzled vest was atop a white cuffed red shirt; a silver hook protruded from his right sleeve.

"What be your name?"

Staring at the captain's hook, Freddy stammered, "Freddy Griswold."

"There's no Griswold assigned to this expedition. You a stowaway?"

"I don't know. REALLY! Is this part of the initiation?" Freddy said, befuddled.

"You're talking gibberish. Down to the hold with you." The captain yelled, "Brinto, Cassen over here. Take this no count, freeloader, and throw him in with Smith."

"Aye, aye, Cap'n Newport," said sailors Brinto and Cassen. They picked Freddy up by his arms and dragged him along the deck, through a door, down three flights of stairs and threw him into a small windowless room. "You got company, Cap'n Smith."

"What in the name of King James is this?" Captain John Smith growled as he looked at Freddy. "Give me any trouble and I'll cut you up into tiny slivers."

"Got a stowaway, we do. Says his name's Griswold. Cap'n Newport said to throw him in with you …keep you company. Har-har." George Cassen snorted as he checked Captain Smith's shackles.

"Griswold, don't be pullin' no funny business lest I have to shackle you up same's your mate."

Freddy eyed his disheveled cabin mate, a man in his mid-twenties, tangled brown hair, a mustache, beard, wearing a leather vest festooned with gold buttons. Under his vest, Smith wore a heavy blue muslin shirt encrusted with filth from days of wear. His tan britches ended below the knee; black slipper-like boots and knee-high socks adorned his feet.

Freddy reached for the Quell Stone in his pocket and felt the calming power of its presence. "Do you know when the initiation is over 'cause Charles is picking me up at 10. Are we playing a masquerade game?" Freddy said trying to sound brave.

"What you talkin' about?" Smith growled. We're in the hold and if you give them cause, they'll throw you overboard.

Smith cursed, tried to stand, fell back and kicked at the shackles furiously.

"What are you in here for?" Did you kill someone?" Freddy said, still thinking this was part of the initiation ritual.

"Not this time, I didn't. Newport'd better beware." John Smith turned to Freddy and studied him for a second. "What's that garb you got on?" He rubbed the windbreaker.

"My friend Charles gave it to me. It's a windbreaker."

"What in tarnation... West ender, are you?"

"The men will tear that costume off ya in two seconds. Take it off...Hide it. Here, put some tar and grease on your face... your hair too. Ya need to bloody look like an urchin. Atta boy! Ashes under your nails." John Smith leaned back against the wall bracing himself.

Spitting and cursing, Smith again yanked at his shackles. "They're aimin' to hang me. Those lily-livered prats don't know a pig's eye about sailing a ship." He wiped his nose on the sleeve of his shirt then blew it, the green gob shooting out about three feet. A brown rat scurried over to the blob, gulped it down and disappeared into a hole.

Freddy observed what just happened and thought he was going to be sick. "It's not polite blowing your nose like that."

"I don' abide manners an' I don' abide you, neither, you little snit."

"Don't be offended. My Gran-dama is just so particular about etiquette. Anyway, so why are they going to hang you?"

"Jealousy," Captain John Smith boasted. "I've got more experience in my pinkie than the whole lot of them together. Nah, Newport wouldn't listen to me…ran right into a storm. I thought we were goners for sure."

"So what happened?" Freddy asked moving closer.

"It was every John for his self. Our esteemed Captain "One-Hand" Newport locked himself in his cabin," Smith said with disgust. "I took over the ship. The men wanted to turn around and head back to England but I said, 'NO! Sail on!' And God the guider of all good actions did drive us to our desired port which we named Cape Henry."

Freddy stuffed his windbreaker into his pants and finished applying grease, mud, and ashes to his hair. "What happened after that?"

"So the Captains all got together and accused me of startin' a mutiny. They're jealous of me 'cause of my fighting experience. I fought the Turks, in the Long War and I was promoted to captain while fighting in Hungary."

Captain Gosnoll, commander of the *Godspeed,* and Captain Ratcliffe, commander of the *Discovery,*
accused me of insubordination and so here I sit waitin' me sentence. They's sayin' they're goin' to hang me up like a Christmas turkey. 'ells bells! We'll see about that," blasted Captain Smith.

Suddenly a black cat with a white star on its forehead sauntered across the floor and stopped in front of Freddy, seemingly unafraid.

"Don't say a word," whispered John Smith. "That's my little Polly Girl.  She's been keepin' me company.  Quite a ratter she is, too.  She's got seven toes to bring us luck—ship's cat. Here Polly, Polly."

Cautiously, the black cat inched her way over to John Smith and sniffed his outstretched hand.  Polly eyed Freddy for a good long minute before deciding to approach him. Then, with a quick bound, she jumped up onto his shoulder and began nudging and nosing his neck and head.

"Welcome aboard, guv," Polly purred in a Cockney accent.

"Thank you," Freddy answered.

"You're welcome," John Smith replied shaking his head, befuddled.

A rat scurried across the floor and instantly all twenty-eight of Polly's digits propelled her into the air and onto the rat.  She held the rat by the neck until its frantic movement ceased.  With the rat firmly clutched in her teeth, Polly turned to Freddy and said, "Got to get dinner to Dacktyle and me nippers.  I'll be back when we can chat a bit."

"Did you hear that?"  Freddy asked.

"Hear what?"

"The cat.  Polly said she had to get dinner to her kids."

.

"A bloody derelict you are, lad. Cats can't talk no more'n eels can dance a jig. Get a hold of yourself!"

Freddy knew what he had heard and was looking forward to seeing Polly again.

## CHAPTER 19
## JAMESTOWNE

On the morning of April 26, 1607, the lookout in the crow's nest on the good ship *Susan Constant* spotted the capes around the entrance to Chesapeake Bay. Four rivers supplied fresh water to this body of salt water. The Englishmen named these rivers the Potomac, Rappahannock, York, and James. At the entrance to the bay was a cape that Captain Newport dubbed Cape Henry after Prince Henry, King James' son. The ships were anchored and thirty crewmen went ashore to explore.

Captain Smith was curled up asleep in the hold of the *Susan Constant*. Freddy was trying to coax a rat out of its hole with a piece of dried bread.

Polly returned, out of breath and jumped up on Freddy's back, "It's a tragedy that's happened."

Freddy reached back, pried her off his dirty t-shirt, and patted her fur. "What's going on? You look like you've just lost one of your lives."

"Me poor Dacky is lucky to get back alive he is. Cap'n Newport sent a party ashore to investigate the new

172

land...Dacky slipped into the dinghy. While my hubby was investigatin' the woods, our crew was attacked with bows and arrows by the most fearsome lookin' savages. Two of the crew was badly wounded...probably won't make it. Then quick as a wink those bloody savages disappeared back into the forest. You'd better wake the Cap'n and give 'im the news," Polly said.

*This is turning out to be more fun than cowboys and Indians.* Freddy crawled over to John Smith and touched his shoulder. Smith shot up spitting and spraying language as foul as his breath. Freddy told him what he had heard.

"Arrrgh, they got what they deserved. If I was calling the shots this wouldn't have happened," Smith said.

## May 13, 1607

Captain Newport opened the sealed orders from the Virginia Company and read the names of those who would run the colony:

President: Captain Edward Maria Wingfield

Council Members:
- Captain Christopher Newport
- Captain Bartholomew Gosnold
- Captain John Ratcliff
- Captain George Kendall

- Captain John Martin
- Captain John Smith

Captain Newport hit the table with his fist, "God have mercy on us all. Send for Smith," Newport barked.

Sailor Jonas Profit dashed to the hold to give Captain Smith the good news and release him from his shackles. "Cap'n, they's just opened the strong box and your name's listed to be on the council. How'd you wrangle that?" Profit asked as his red blistered hands fumbled with the lock.

"Get the bloomin' chains off, Profit. I've a thing or two to say to those know-nothin' twits."

"Come on Freddy, let's get this settled." Captain Smith bounded up the stairs to the captain's quarters, burst in without knocking, yelling, "You will rue the day you locked me up depriving me of my rightful duty to command this venture." He spit on the cabin floor.

Freddy was excited by all the commotion. He wondered if there'd be a rumble.

"SILENCE!" Captain Newport ordered. "You are an overbearing, hot-tempered insubordinate. Your crude, irascible demeanor makes you unfit for service to the king. By the power vested in me as commander of this ship, I declare that you, John Smith, be taken back to England and

174

tried for mutiny and insubordination which is punishable by hanging. If there be any man against this action, stand now."

The captains in attendance, (Wingfield, Gosnold, Ratcliffe, Kendall and Martin) remained seated.

"Then let it be noted that Captain John Smith is hereby arrested and is to be shackled until such time as I can return to England. Profit, return this man to the hold."

Freddy who had been listening in the hallway made a hurried retreat back to the hold.

Freddy was petting Polly when Captain Smith was unceremoniously thrown back into the cell. "They'll be needin' me, you can be sure, and beggin' for me help before you can say Jack Sprat." Captain Smith spit out his words.

"Captain, Polly has been talking to me and telling me all about herself and her family. Her husband's name's Dactyle and her two kittens are named Boots and Cricket. Look at Boots…so cute…looks like his mother. Cricket's a bit shy, though. Ask Polly something. See if she'll talk to you."

"Oh, awright. How'd you get on board?"

"Well, Cap'n, it's like this," Polly said thoughtfully. "Me man and me was livin' in White Chapel on the east end of London.  Slimy, filthy place it is…nothin' but chicken bones. Starvin' we was."

Dactyle appeared from underneath a stack of tools, stretched his legs, sharpened his claws, shook his orange body, and scratched behind his ear. Tufts of fur flew like a dandelion top caught in a breeze. "Wot's goin' on, me wifie darlin'?"

"Jus tellin about the old days at the Blind Beggar, luv.  As I was sayin', we was half dead when this bloke comin' out of the pub picked me up.  He turned me over and noticed that I'm polydactyl, ya know…have seven toes. Then he took a gander at me dear hubby's paws.  This bugger got so excited.  He scooped us up and took us into the pub and ordered a saucer of milk for the both of us.  He was tellin ever' one that we bring luck to a ship cause we got seven toes," Polly said as she held up her paw.

Pacing back and forth and rubbing Captain Smith's legs and then Freddy's, Dactyle gloated, "That's when our luck changed, mate.  This bloke turns out to be Cap'n Newport, commander of the *Susan Constant* which was settin' to sail in December for the New World.  So he brought us aboard ship and it's been good victuals all the way. Enough rats for a family of four, to be sure."

Freddy glanced over at the captain but he was sound asleep.

Freddy looked worried. *"I wonder when this initiation is going to be over? Charles is going to be so mad when I'm not back at the Rexall on time."*

## May 14, 1607

Captain Newport decided to lay anchor forty miles from the mouth of the Chesapeake Bay on an island they named Jamestowne in honor of King James of England. The area was marshy and infested with mosquitoes; the worst possible place to moor their ships. Captain Newport ordered the men off the ship to begin working. The ground was nothing but wet slop. It was hard going for the workers who were slipping and falling in the muck. An area was cleared away from the marshiest part. Some men cut down trees to make a place to pitch their tents; others began building the fort or tilling the ground for planting. In the beginning the colonists survived primarily on fish and turtles. When the sun went down, balls of mosquitoes attacked and shrouded the men. The itching, bleeding sores covered their bodies. Many men grew sick and some died of malaria.

Dactyle took Boots and Cricket to the woods for hunting lessons. Polly stayed on the ship with shackled Captain Smith and Freddy.

"Me Dacky says the sight on the island is jus pi'iful. Cap'n should take a butcher's at the posh gents runnin' roun' in them puffy britches, wearin' them high-heeled boots and their hoity toity hats with feathers," Polly purred in Freddy's ear.

Captain Smith looked at Freddy and announced, "This whole expedition is doomed for failure if the gents don't get to working alongside the laborers. Can you figure? Forty-eight able bodied men all dressed up in their glad rags poking around, looking for gold, writing in their journals, expecting to be waited on. Arrhh! If I was in command I'd get some blisters on their hands for sure." Captain Smith yanked at his shackles.

"Captain Smith, it's been a very exciting adventure," Freddy said, "but I think I should go home now."

"Freddy, you can't go home. This is your home now unless you get kicked off. You shouldn't have sneaked on board in the first place," Captain Smith scoffed. *Youth! Don't know when they's well off.*

"This is too weird," Freddy said. "I know this is part of the initiation but it's gone on way too long. It's not funny anymore."

Smith said, "Well you should ov thought about that before you slipped on this rigger. If I get out of here, you can be me sidekick. Now wouldn't that be something?"

Freddy went to the supply room and brought back some hard tack and a mug of ale for Captain Smith. "The ale's getting low. I guess most everyone is drinking from the river by now," Freddy said.

Captain Smith growled, "It won't stay fresh long if the blokes don't fix up a proper place to relieve themselves, ya know."

"I think I should help do something, like cutting down trees for the fort." Freddy said. "I met Samuell Collier and Richard Mutton...about my age, from London... said they needed more help. There's only sixteen men, them included, that are doing the hard labor to prepare for winter."

"If Newport knows what good for him, he'd better order these chains off and give me a command." Captain Smith was petting Polly. "Isn't that right Polly girl?" Polly purred; her eyes closed.

Freddy was thinking that this place might not be so bad after all. He was making friends and having a great adventure.

## May 26, 1607

Freddy scuttled down the stairs to the hold. He was out of breath. "Captain Smith, Captain Smith! We've just been attacked. I heard it was the Powhatans. They killed Henry Tavin and William Unger. Ten others are badly wounded."

"Criminy! Did we get any savages?"

"I don't think so. It happened so suddenly. By the time the men found their guns the savages had already disappeared back into the forest." Freddy said his eyes big as saucers.

# CHAPTER 20
# CAPTAIN SMITH TAKES CHARGE

The Captains Wingfield, Gosnoll, Ratliffe, Martin, Newport, and Kendall met inside the partially completed fort. Squatting in the grass, Wingfield was the first to speak. "If we don't do something quick we're going to be destroyed. The only one that really knows how to communicate with these savages is Smith. I say we release him."

And so it was agreed. Captain John Smith was now free and took his rightful place in the council. It was noted by many of the colonists that the commanders had spread lies concerning John Smith because of their jealousy and envy of his previous experience.

\*\*\*\*\*\*

The attacks by the Powhatan Indians continued. Surprisingly though, there were times when the Indians approached peacefully bringing food to the settlers in exchange for copper and iron implements. At last the wooden palisaded fort was complete. It was built in a triangular shape around a storehouse, a church and a number of houses. The settlers now had some sense of protection.

Freddy was really getting worried. He felt like he had been gone for days. He wondered if anyone was searching for him.

****** 

After the fort was completed, Captain Smith and Captain "One Hand" Newport organized an exploratory trip to the headwaters of the James River. Eighteen seamen and gents, along with Freddy, boarded the barge. It was a cool, crisp morning, the water placid. One of the gents, Francis Snarsbrough, was writing in his journal and drawing pictures of the wildlife along the river banks. Freddy watched him for a while, and then said, "Are you enjoying the trip?"

Snarsbrough stopped writing and said, "You are very impertinent, young man. How dare someone of your class speak to me. I should have you whipped."

"Well I was only trying to make conversation. Besides, I know something about you."

"I daresay, a guttersnipe like you would know nothing about me." Snarsbrough removed his hat, waving it at Freddy like he was shoeing away gnats. Freddy noted that under his hat Snarsbrough had a rooster tail sticking up.

"Go on about your business and leave me alone," Snarsbrough said as he looked at the gents who were listening. "A bit nervy of this gutter rat."

"I happen to know that you are my great, great, great grandfather and I was named after you," Freddy said smugly.

"They need to put you in the brig for making up such whopping tales." Snarsbrough called to Captain Smith, "Captain, keep your boy away from me…he's quite brash and doesn't know his place."

"Freddy, leave Sir Snarsbrough alone. Come up here and help me look for signs of savages."

Freddy muttered, "I don't want to be related to you either…what an arse. I bet Gran-dama would give you a tongue lashing if she were here."

## CHAPTER 21
## KING POWHATAN

The first English expedition explored the James River. They passed small native villages hidden in the lush greenery. After three days, the explorers arrived at a village pleasantly seated on a hill with twelve houses called yehakins. The yehakins were covered with reed made from saplings of native trees. They were located near fields planted with corn, beans and squash.

Before docking the barge, Captain Smith advised the men to be respectful and to proceed with caution. "It looks like the chief and his warriors are coming to greet us. Everyone smile and for heaven's sake act calm," Smith said as he stepped off the boat.

Leading the Indian party was a tall, imposing man adorned with necklaces of bear claws and beaver teeth; he wore a loin cloth of deer hide and a stern, sour look. Behind him were a group of twenty warriors.

John Smith, flanked by his entourage, stepped forward. He raised his hand, palm open. "I am John Smith. We come in peace"

The Indian man stood solidly in place; his arms crossed. He looked at Smith with eyes of steel, and waited.

Captain Smith returned the stare and waited.

No one moved.

"I am Chief," the leader answered flatly. "My village."

Captain Smith assumed this was the Great Emperor Powhatan. Soon he learned that every village had a ruling chief and that they were all Powhatans. They would not meet the Great Emperor for many days.

"Come. Let us talk in my yehakin."

"Freddy, mingle with the youngsters. Maybe, they'll let you in on one of their games," Captain Smith said as followed the Chief to his yehakin.

Freddy reached in his pocket, rubbed the Quell Stone and felt courageous enough to venture over to a group of braves playing a game with a stick and a round shaped object covered in deer hide. Freddy approached the boys and raised his palm. "Using crude sign language, Freddy told them his name was Freddy. The boys spent a while trying to pronounce Freddy's name. One of the braves smiled at Freddy and said his name was Kitchi. Kitchi gestured for Freddy to join them in their game. Freddy caught on quickly.

After they tired of the game, Kitchi and several braves motioned for Freddy to follow them. They ran through the forest, zigzagging though the tall trees and underbrush. Freddy had to stop to get his breath but the braves kept running. Soon, he didn't see any signs of his friends.

Freddy called out, "Kitchi" No answer. Freddy listened and heard many sounds of forest life. A group of birds exploded out of the nearby tall grass.

Freddy could feel a sense of panic welling up. *I don't know which way to go. I'm lost.* He fell to the ground wondering why his friends had abandoned him.

In the distance, Freddy heard, "Caw! Caw! Caw! Caw!" And then out of the brush burst Kitchi and the others, laughing.

Freddy was not laughing. He held his hands out indicating, "Why, did you leave me?"

Kitchi gestured for Freddy to follow him to a tree where a turtle was etched in the bark. Then he took Freddy to another tree where a turtle was etched. They went from tree to tree following the turtle signs. Soon they emerged from the forest and they were back at the village.

This was a very important lesson Freddy learned. He felt he had gained a new skill that could be very useful in the future.

Then he paused in his thoughts... *This is the most fun I've had since Mama...*and he felt a twinge of guilt. He closed his eyes and visualized playing ball with his mother.

John Smith and Captain Newport entered the yehakin behind the Chief and his sub-chiefs. The yehakin was roomy and much larger than Smith expected. Wooden benches covered with deer skin lined the inside walls. Poles securing the structure held baskets, animal skins, and cooking pots. In the center of the room a fire was flickering, warming the earthen floor and interior space.

The Chief, Smith, and Newport seated themselves around the fire; the sub-chiefs stood. Captain Newport spoke first.

"My people have been having much trouble with a group of savages that call themselves the Paspahegh. We have done nothing to them yet they come to our village and attack us with their bows and arrows and have killed several of our men. We just want peace. Captain Smith and I want to make an alliance with you against the Paspahegh."

The Chief's eyes blazed with fire. He stood. "You have come to insult me. The Paspahegh are my brothers. I am Powhatan— the Paspahegh, the Chickahominy, the Mattaponi, are Powhatan. We number twenty thousand men."

Captain John Smith stood up and began to employ his skill as an arbitrator. "I think you have misunderstood, Great Chief. What my brother was trying to say was that we need your skill and knowledge to plant corn, hunt deer, prepare the meat and catch the fish—and certainly to make friends with your brothers. We want to live in peace with you and your people."

Captain Smith presented a scarlet cloak, a clock and tools to Chief Powhatan. The Chief was quite taken with the clock and wanted to know what it was for and what made the ticking sound.

For the time being a truce had been stuck.

******

The Powhatan village chief invited the Englishmen to stay the night and eat with the tribe. They gathered in an open area where the meal was being prepared. The women of the village were engaged in many activities. A few were tending the fire; others were baking corn cakes while some were cleaning the ground around the fire. A young girl, hair braided and adorned with beads, carried a water-filled clay pot on her head. She set it next to the women grinding corn. Her body was tattooed with both flowers and a coiled snake that wound around and up her arm; her face was painted with a mixture of red paint and nut oil to keep insects away. Around her waist was an apron made of deerskin decorated with fringe. Long necklaces made of shells and animal bones hung from her neck. None of the women looked at the men. Their gaze remained on the task at hand.

Large clay pots filled with stew simmered on coals. Freddy stared at the turkey roasting on a spit over the open fire. "Captain Smith, when do we get to eat? The smell of the turkey is making me as hungry as a big old bear."

"I hope it's soon, Freddy. I'm famished," Captain Smith replied.

The Chief motioned for all to sit. Captain Smith and Freddy sat next to the great leader. The women served the men in clay bowls. Freddy gulped down his meal and lifted his bowl for more.

John Smith chided Freddy, "We are their guests. Don't appear greedy and unappreciative. We have to be very careful we don't offend them."

Freddy said, "I just thought they would be pleased that I wanted more."

Captain Smith leaned over to Freddy and whispered, "That is not their custom. Guests have to be respectful and wait to be offered more."

After the sumptuous meal, the men smoked pipes that served to seal the bond of friendship. When the pipe was passed to Freddy, he sat like the others and took a draw. He coughed and his throat burned. Soon he began to feel relaxed and dreamy. The Powhatan village leader and the others smiled and nodded their heads. Freddy had the sensation he was floating and could see St. Wigbod and Mrs. McVicker in the kitchen. He had an intense longing to return home.

Without warning, the Chief stood and walked away to his yehakin. His sub-chiefs motioned for Captain Smith and his party to follow them. Two yehakins or longhouses were indicated for the Englishmen to sleep. The houses were a single room where frames for sleeping lined the inside walls. Deer skins were stacked high in one corner. A smoke hole cut in the roof directly over the fire provided ventilation for the room.

"This has been quite a day, huh, Captain Smith?" Freddy was getting a deer skin. "Can I bring you one, sir?"

"I'd be much obliged." Captain Smith took the animal skin, curled up on the bench and yawned. Freddy made his bed on the ground next to Smith. The night noises kept Freddy awake and he couldn't get comfortable. Just as he was drifting off, Freddy was startled by the sound of sniffing and digging outside the yehakin.

Freddy screamed, "Mama!"

Captain Smith reached down and patted Freddy, "You're having a bad dream, lad. Go to sleep."

Freddy felt homesick, put his hands to his face and softly whimpered.

******

The morning dawned a misty gray. The party of Englishmen boarded their barge after paying tribute to the Chief and the sub-chiefs. An Indian brave ran up to the barge as it was being pushed away from the shore. He threw a deerskin ball to Freddy.

The boy yelled "Kemotte!" meaning brother.

Freddy held up the ball.

"Kenagh, kenagh. Thank you, Kitchi." Freddy looked at Captain Smith, "His name's Kitchi. It means brave." Freddy waved the ball shouting "Kemotte, kemotte!"

The barge drifted downstream while Kitchi grew smaller and smaller. A feeling of sadness enveloped Freddy. He knew he was going to miss the freedom and friendship he had felt at the village.

Captain Smith smiled, "It looks like you made a friend."

Freddy nodded and his eyes welled up.

Loaded with corn, deer hides, nuts, grains and other edible plants, the explorers headed back to Jamestowne. They had been gone for seven days.

As the barge neared Jamestowne, Edward Brinto, builder and mason, ran down to the bank hollering, "Captain Smith! We were attacked! The savages killed Eustace Clovill."

The barge slammed onto the shore. Men jumped out, sloshed through the water and mud, ran to the fort where they faced the aftermath of the brutal attack. The injured had arrows in their arms, legs, torso, and back. The ground was flowing red with blood.

"Who did this?" yelled Captain Newport.

"Get these wounded inside the fort," ordered Captain John Smith.

"About two hundred savages ambushed us more'n an hour ago," Edward Brinto said, dragging a wounded man into the fort. "Most of us were inside except'n these miserable souls out tending the garden when the savages attacked from over there in the tall grass. Before you know'd it we was surrounded. By the time the men got to their guns the bloody savages had disappeared."

Freddy was confounded. *This is gruesome. I thought we were friends with the Indians. Kitchi and I played together. Why would they do this?*

The injured who were carried inside the fort had their wounds attended to by Thomas Wotton, the Chirurg or surgeon. Freddy assisted him by bringing wet rags and covering the wounds with strips of cloth to stop the bleeding. Half of these men died from infection or malnourishment.

# CHAPTER 22
## NIGHT HUNTS

L ife for Freddy at Jamestowne was hard work but it was also an adventure. During the day he cleared the area of tall grass, carried logs inside the palisade, and fished. He lodged with Captain Smith in a tent inside the fort – his castle on the ground. At night Polly slept with Freddy, keeping him warm, while Dactyle and the twins, roamed the woods in search of food ——rats, birds, and other small animals.

Freddy was awakened by a steady scratching on the flap of the tent one night in late June. Groggily he whispered to Polly, "Go see if that's Dactyle back from his midnight hunt."

"Oh a'right. I'll see to it. Dacky, is that you, luv?"

"No, Mum, it's me, Cricket. Papa and Boots caught the most awful things and they's bringin' um home. Let me in," Cricket mewed.

Presently Dactyle and Boots entered the tent triumphantly. They laid down their booty. Before you could say Henry Horntoad, the hideous beasts began squealing, their large eyes gleaming with fright, their open mouths reflecting razor sharp teeth.  Flip, flop – the furry creatures took flight inside the tent, darting here, darting there, and crashing into one side of the tent and then the other.   Dactyle and Boots leaped, lurched, lunged, just missing the flying winged creatures.

"Blimy, wot's goin' on?" yelled Polly.

"Don't worry, Mum, ever'thing's under control," Boots said as he twisted and swatted at the frightened darting things.

Startled out of his sleep John Smith murmured, "What in the name of King James is going on?"

"Dactyle and Boots brought um in.  What are they?" Freddy asked hovering in the corner with Polly.

"Oh, this place's gone barmy.  For goodness sakes they've brought in bats.  Stay calm.  We've got to get them out and back to their night affairs…eating mosquitoes."

Freddy threw the cats out; Captain Smith threw his cover over the bats clinging to the side of the tent, wrapped them up and then released them into the night.  The bats quickly gained their composure and then lickety split took flight zigzagging into the sky and out of sight.

Growling, Captain Smith said, "Darn cats.  If it weren't for Newport I'd throw the lot of them in the river."

195

# Chapter 23
## Unrest at the Fort

**June 22, 1607**

Captain Newport departed Jamestowne for England having completed his mission to navigate the settlers to the new world. He took a crew of thirty to man the *Susan Constant* and the *Godspeed,* leaving the smaller ship *Discovery* for the colonists. The provisions from the *Discovery* were distributed to those left behind. Unfortunately, the grain had been setting and roasting inside the ship for six weeks. Nicholas Houlgrave opened a sack and was immediately nauseated from the stench of rot and maggots.

"We can't eat this!" yelled Houlgrave. "What will we eat? We're sure to starve."

The men became angry and defiant. "Since Cap'n Newport left and took the ale, we don't have nothin' to drink."

"We've been abandoned," shouted another settler.

Freddy was getting anxious seeing how desperate the men had become. *I hope Captain Smith can use his charm and diplomacy to settle the men down.*

Captain John Smith tried to calm the agitated men. "We need to work together to make our gardens produce. Every able-bodied man must work in order to eat. We have some *gentlemen* who think they're too good to do a day's labor. You may have been gentry in England but not here. Remember lads, you reap what you sow. Every man will work from dawn to dusk. You will hunt, fish, gather berries and till the soil so that we can survive until Captain Newport returns with the first supply."

For the time being the men were pacified.

## August 1607

The extreme heat, poor nutrition, and hard labor were taking a toll on the colonists. The river was polluted, full of slime and filth. The men were suffering from dysentery, typhoid fever and other mosquito-borne illnesses. John Asbie died of the bloody flux, George Flowers died from the swelling and William Bruster died from the wound he received from an attack by the natives. At times there were only five able-bodied men to bury the dead. In all, fifty died.

The leadership of the colony was deteriorating.

## September 10, 1607

Captain Wingfield was found guilty of libel, was deposed as president of the colony and replaced by Captain Ratcliff. After Captain Bartholomew Gosnell died, Captain George Kendall was convicted of conspiracy. Before he was shot, Kendall proclaimed that President Ratcliff was using an assumed name and that his real name was John Sicklemore.

Of the original seven council members, three were now left— Smith, Martin, and Ratcliff.

Food was scarce and those left at Jamestowne would have surely died except for the mercy of the natives who apparently had a change of heart. They brought life-saving food and other provisions to the forty-eight left at the fort.

# CHAPTER 24
## SAVAGE ENCOUNTERS

**December 10, 1607**

The bitter cold in Jamestowne made each day a struggle for survival. They were scraping the bottom of the barrels for any remnants that might be present. Captain Smith decided to take Freddy and ten men along with his Indian guide on a food gathering expedition up the Chickahominy River. Snow covered the ground on this overcast December day. The men paddled the barge carefully along the partially frozen river until they saw a herd of deer nibbling on the last of the vegetation; swans, ducks and geese filled the river. The barge was silently guided to the riverbank.

Captain Smith quietly ordered, "Cassen! Emry! After the deer! See to it you bag one." The others began shooting river fowl.

Suddenly, out of the mist came hellish shrieks, "Yieoh, eewooh! Opaivwh minatew nagadan!" (White man leave!) Three hundred savages appeared from the forest, running, shooting arrows, bent on killing.

Captain Smith grabbed his Indian guide and, using him as a shield, retreated to the river before slipping into its bitterly cold water. Freddy ran after them rubbing his Quell Stone and felt its protective energy propelling him at lightning speed. He dove into the frigid river narrowly escaping an arrow.

Lips blue and limbs numb, they felt the sting of death approaching. They abandoned their weapons and called for help. A tall native named Opechankanough (O-pa-CHAN-ca-no) ordered his men to rescue John Smith, his guide, and Freddy. Two Englishmen had been slain and the others wounded. The warriors lead Captain Smith, Freddy and his guide to a campfire where Smith's men and his guide were slain. Freddy and John Smith were each tied to a tree. Customarily, the Indians built a fire around the tree and roasted their captives. Freddy was gritting his teeth and wondering if this was where he was going to die.

John Smith looked at Freddy as he spoke, "I suppose this is the end, lad…you have proved your courage."

Two warriors were approaching the tree with lighted torches.

"Captain, I have a Quell Stone. It protects me and gives me strength whenever I rub it. I'll try to get a hold of it in my pocket." Freddy's fingers reached, stretched and gradually inched forward—little by little he strained until his finger tips felt the Quell Stone. With one great force of effort his fingers grabbed the stone. He rubbed its smooth surface and felt its magical powers surging through his body. The rope tying Freddy to the tree untwisted and exploded from his body, sending twine spinning like a tornado.

The warriors dropped their torches and pulled back.

"Freddy," Captain Smith called, "I have a compass in my pocket. Get it out. Show it to the leader." Freddy reached into his pants' pocket and pulled out the ivory compass.

Holding the compass, Freddy got the attention of two braves, aghast by what had just happened. Freddy held the compass out for them to see. Cautiously they approached. They were wary but fascinated and marveled at the fly and needle which they could see but not touch. The commotion brought King Opechankanough to investigate. He, too, became enchanted by the compass and for an hour the savages played with this curious instrument. Then, tiring of their diversion, the warriors encircled Captain Smith and prepared to set him on fire.

Freddy rubbed the Quell Stone and repeated the mantra, "For whatever is good and praiseworthy we will be protected." A magnificent display of silver and gold sparks shot up and lite the night sky.

The braves covered their eyes, and dropped to the ground.

Opechankanough shouted, "STOP! They have magic." Holding the compass he said, "We take to village. Put down fire."

"That was close," Freddy murmured.

Captain Smith and Freddy were lead through the woods by several braves. Soon they came to a village with about twenty hunting houses made of straw mats. Tribal warriors formed a ring and began dancing, singing and shrieking fearsome cries. Their faces, heads and shoulders were painted red and each wore either fox or otter skins around their arms. Captain Smith and Freddy stood with King Opechankanough in the middle of the dancing warriors. In one hand the chief held his bow and in the other his arrows. On his head the feathers of an eagle were fastened into a headdress; around his neck were pieces of copper, white shells, feathers and the rattles of snakes. After three dances the warriors departed and Smith and Freddy were taken to a long house where they were fed a meal of bread and venison. Twenty tall warriors guarded them and at times mocked them. Freddy felt insecure and afraid that at any moment  he and Captain Smith could be killed.

Freddy remembered the Quell Stone and wondered if it had the power to take him back home. He felt it in his pocket but was afraid the guards might see it and take it away.  Carefully, he took the stone from his pocket, held it in the palm of this hand and rubbed it over and over. Nothing happened—he was still in the yehakin with Captain Smith.  However, his fear was quelled and his mind drifted to Wiggins' Preparatory. *Maybe if I give school a try, things will get better. Mrs. McVicker said that hardships can actually make you stronger. She might be right.*

They were kept in the yehakin for two days as the tribal warriors performed their rituals.

On the third day, a man with the intention to slay Captain Smith appeared at the village. His son lay sick and dying from gunshot wounds he had received from Captain Smith's men back at the James River.

The anguished man was screaming and spitting at Captain Smith.  He held a tomahawk and was ready to use it.

Captain Smith pleaded, "I have magic water back at the fort that can heal your son.  Let me go and get it,"

"No, you bad people. We no trust. We kill you and destroy fort," answered the native.

"Listen to me. I can save your son. Let me send my son to get the magic water," Smith said, pointing to Freddy. "We have many supplies that we can give to you if you will be patient and trust me."

The native man finally agreed. John Smith made an inventory of items he wanted and listed them on a paper. He gave Freddy the message to take to the fort. Immediately Freddy and ten braves set out for the fort at Jamestowne in the bitter cold of frost and snow. The braves led the way following paths and signs on trees they had made to keep from getting lost. When they reached their destination, the Indians hid in the forest while Freddy went inside the fort and delivered the message.

To the natives' surprise the requested items appeared outside the fort the following morning. The Indians surmised that either the English Captain must have divine power or that the paper could talk.

When the native men returned to their village with Freddy in tow, they regaled the Captain and Freddy with feasts and entertainment. The native man was given life saving medicine to heal his son.

A great fire was made in the long house, mats spread out, and the two prisoners ordered to sit. Soon a fearsome warrior came before them painted all over with a mixture of coal and oil. On his head was a crown formed by the tails of snakes and weasels. Around the crown was a coronet of feathers; skins of animals hung round his head covering his face, back and shoulders. With rattles in his hand he contorted in strange gestures and began an incantation, his voice like a banshee.

Then three devil-like creatures painted half black and half red rushed into the center of the room; their eyes painted white and streaks of red paint cut across their cheeks. Their ritualistic dance became a fiendish frenzy. Three more savages came in with painted faces, dancing, and undulating, seemingly possessed by demons until they finished in a rushing crescendo. All sat down—half on either side of the Chief Priest. At the Priest's signal his legion began shaking rattles, singing and chanting. When the song ended the priest laid five ears of corn around the fire. With his arms extended above his head, the priest began swaying with a mighty force, pounding the ground with such violence that the veins in his hand swelled and a great sweat spilled from his body. Afterwards the priest rose and gave a short oration; at its end the men gave a low, quick grunt—UGH! Once again the men shook their rattles and sang. Again, the priest lay down five ears of corn and repeated all he had done before. This ceremony lasted until nightfall. At no time did anyone eat or drink. At the end of the night Captain Smith and Freddy were offered food and drink and all who had partaken in the ritual feasted with great merriment. For three days this ceremony continued. Freddy was exhausted from lack of sleep and the desire to get back home.

The priest said to Smith, "You have passed great test; you have shown you are netoppew (friend)."

Captain Smith answered, "Mawchick Chammay—the best of friends."

The next day Opitchapan, the King's brother, took Freddy and Captain Smith to his yehakin where they were warmly welcomed and invited to partake of a feast—bread, turkey, pheasant, and many kinds of vegetables. Captain Smith and Freddy, however dined alone; none of Opitchapan's household was allowed to eat with the white men. When the captain and Freddy had eaten sufficiently, the table was cleared and the leftover food put in baskets. That evening John Smith and Freddy were led back to the village of King Opechankanough, carrying the baskets of food.

Accompanying them were ten braves. It was nightfall when the party approached the village; children ran to greet Freddy and Smith, cheering and screaming with joy.

Grabbing a basket filled with corncakes, a native boy of seven years cried, "Mowchick weyawgh tawgh!" (I am very hungry). Cries of "Noughmas!" (fish) and "Netoppew!" (friends) were chanted throughout the village. After a while the native children returned to their running games; Freddy and the captain were led to their yehakin.

Freddy could not sleep that night because Captain Smith seemed to be having nightmares. He thrashed and screamed torturous howls. His body shook, twisted, and flailed. Sweat poured from his body.

"Captain Smith," Freddy whispered as he shook the captain's shoulder. "Wake up. You're having a bad dream."

Startled, Captain Smith sat up rigid as a board. He struck at Freddy, hitting him in his jaw. "Freddy, thank goodness. I was having the most grotesque dream. Demons appeared. They hissed, spit, and snarled. Their yellow teeth curled out from their lips, ripped my flesh and devoured it. My blood spew upon the ground and they lapped it up while gazing at me with eyes blazing fire and their nostrils belching smoke. One demon held a key which opened an abyss. Pouring forth from the abyss was black smoke filled with locusts. The locusts became scorpions stinging all within their reach."

"Captain! How frightening!" Freddy thought of his fear of scorpions and shivered. "You have had so much worry. Also, some of the food you ate at Opitchapan's yehakin last night might have caused these dreams."

Reaching into his pants' pocket, Freddy felt the Quell Stone and pulled it out. He handed the black smooth rock to Smith and said, "Rub this stone and think about whatever is noble, true and right. As you rub this stone you will feel a lightness and sense of strength that will amaze you."

Captain Smith took the stone and rubbed it. A calming sense of well-being spread over him. The stone changed from black to white. Sparks of lightening bounced off the stone and disappeared into thin air.

"This Quell Stone is magical. Do you have another one?"

"No sir, I'm afraid not. I'd give it to you but I think I may need it to get back home again."

Freddy lay back down on the cold ground and wrapped himself in the deerskin. *When am I going home? I just want to go home.*

Freddy could smell Mrs. McVicker's biscuits as he drifted off to sleep.

# CHAPTER 24
# POCAHONTAS SAVES JOHN SMITH

For the next two weeks, Freddy and Captain John Smith were herded from one Indian village to another. They were greeted with hospitality from the village of Werowocomoco (Werowoco-mo-co) on the York River to the village of Tappahannock (TAPP-ah-HANN-ock) on the Rappahannock River (rap-uh-HANN-ock) and numerous other villages in between.

Captain Smith and Freddy learned that The Great Emperor Powhatan, leader of all the chiefdoms, had many villages in the land around the James River. He also had many wives who attended to his every need.

**December 29, 1607**

The weather had turned extremely wet and cold.

"I am so thankful our Indian friends gave us these deerskins to keep us from freezing to death," Freddy said, shivering.

John Smith noticed Freddy lining his shoes with soft deerskin. "It's a good thing you made friends with Kitchi. His ball has come in handy."

Exhausted from traveling over one hundred miles on foot, Freddy and Smith were brought to Meronocomo where the Great Emperor Powhatan was residing. Guarding his great house were two hundred grim faced warriors.

Freddy gathered his deer hide tightly around his shoulders. "Captain, do you think these guys are friendly?"

Captain Smith said, "By the expressions on their faces, I'd say they don't seem any too happy to see us. Keep your Quell Stone handy. We're probably going to need it."

Captain Smith and Freddy were roughly pushed through the middle of these grim faced courtiers, and into a great hall. On both sides of the room sat two rows of men, their heads and shoulders painted red; in their hair were the downy feathers of colorful birds. About their necks were chains of white beads. Behind the men sat as many women.

The Emperor entered with his Queen Appamatuck. The people gave a loud shout. The ruler ceremoniously paraded around the room to a high-back chair carved of dark wood where he sat upon his throne. The queen brought Emperor Powhatan water from a ceremonial jar. He washed his hands and then dried them on a nest of feathers used for high ritualistic purposes. When all was done Queen Appamatuck took her position at the right of her king.

The courtiers and the emperor gathered together and entered into prolonged consultation.

Freddy was very curious. *I wonder what they are discussing.*

With great fanfare, the royal attendants departed and returned with two enormous stones which they placed before their leader. "Bring the man Smith and place him on the stones," the Emperor commanded. Many warriors laid their hands on Smith and dragged him to the stones where they positioned his head on top. At the order of Powhatan, his soldiers raised their clubs in readiness for the command to bludgeon the life from Captain John Smith.

Freddy felt numb and helpless. *This can't be happening after all we've been through. I've got to do something. The Quell Stone!* Freddy found it deep in his pocket and tried to retrieve it, but it kept slipping from his grasp.

.

In desperation he rubbed the stone on the small part he could feel and softly spoke the mantra, "Ponder on what is good, noble, and right."

Without warning, a young girl rose up from the feet of Emperor Powhatan and proceeded to John Smith where she knelt and covered his head with hers. She looked over at her father, extending her willowy arms and said, "Dearest father and great emperor, I beg of you to spare this man's life."

She was the emperor's favored eleven-year-old daughter, Matoaka, whom they called Pocahontas, meaning playful one.

Powhatan leaned to his wife in discussion. He stood, held his royal spear high and pronounced, "Dear Pocahontas, your wish has been granted. This man's life I mercifully spare."

Freddy ran to John Smith extending his hand and helped him up. Freddy spoke as one who had grown in learning and understanding. "Captain, I used the Quell Stone to think of what is good and noble. At that moment the emperor's daughter had the strength and courage to beg for your life. It seems when we think of the good in life our lives can be changed."

Captain John Smith looked at Freddy with gentle eyes. "If I ever have a son I'd hope he'd be just like you."

.

The following day, ten warriors entered Smith's yehakin bringing food and clay pots filled with water.

"Eat and wash body," said a somber-faced brave. "Our Emperor wishes to see you and son."

Captain Smith and Freddy were then led to a great house in the woods where they were left unattended. Then, from outside came the most doleful noise, not unlike the mourner's song. The sorrowful sounds continued unabated for what seemed like hours and then abruptly stopped.

Emperor Powhatan entered the house accompanied by two hundred men with the appearance of devils painted altogether black.

Extending his arms in friendship Powhatan said, "We are now friends, Captain Smith. You and your son may return to Jamestowne. I will forever esteem you as my own son."

"You are a great and mighty leader," John Smith said, extending his arms in friendship.

The mighty Emperor Powhatan said, "Go now in peace!"

# Chapter 25
# Traitors at Jamestowne

**January 2, 1608**

And so, Captain Smith and Freddy were escorted by twelve guides back to Jamestowne. The fear of death at the hands of the Powhatans remained in Freddy's heart until they at last reached the Jamestowne fort. The Powhatans were given gifts of toys, beads and two guns to take back to Emperor Powhatan, his women and children. Then, Captain Smith and Freddy bid their escorts *adieu*. "Thank you," Freddy said. "We enjoyed your hospitality."

As the Indians disappeared into the forest, a scrambling of cats racing at lightning speed sped toward Freddy. There was a cacophony of screeches and wails.

"Tell the Cap'n to save his self. Ratcliff and his ruffians are aimin' to hang him up like a Christmas goose," Dactyle shrieked.

"They's been plottin' for days, they have," echoed Boots. "Those grotty, wasters blame Cap'n for the deaths of the men. Before you got back they was fixin to cast off for England on the *Discovery*. They's barmy to take off in that dinghy."

Captain Ratcliff and four rangy, emaciated men ran at Captain Smith and threw him off balance. As he fell backwards, Smith hit his head on a rock and blacked out.

\*\*\*\*\*\*

When he came to, he was bound up with rope, lying in a small dark hole.

"Well, lookie what's become of the great adventurer," Captain Ratcliff said to Freddy. "You'd better choose your fate, boy," Ratcliff sneered. "Hang with us or you'll surely hang with Smith at dawn."

Ratcliff was fondly stroking his new pet, Lister Rattus. "See here, my dear Lister," Ratcliff hissed, "go down into the hole and nibble an ear for your dinner." Captain Ratcliff threw the rat onto Smith who kicked frantically. Lister Rattus lifted his head sniffing the air for an open wound. With teeth bared the rat plunged onto his victim's face.

"Hold on, guv! We're comin' to your rescue." Stampeding through the grass, Dactyle, Boots, and Cricket lunged into the hole. Lister Rattus reared up on his back legs, mouth open, yellow fangs protruding. Bloody red tears squirted from his eyes, splattering across Captain Smith's mouth.

"Pinch his tail, lads. That'll send him out looking for food," Dactyle ordered. The hole was ablaze with tail pinching and high pitched squealing.

"I can't take no more. I gotta find something to eat," Lister Rattus said, as he bolted up and out of the hole.

Dactyle said, "Good work, me lads. The old tail squeeze works every time. Now let's get the Cap'n untied and back to business."

Reaching into the hole, Freddy lifted Dactyle out.

"Where's Polly? She alright?" Freddy asked.

"Ah, yes. Me Polly is at home with the little ones, ya know. Whilst you was gone a huntin' we added to our family." Dactyle was beaming. "Yes, sir…two beautiful daughters and three strong lads. Lawd, this new country is bringin' me abundance."

Remembering that Captain Smith was still in the hole, Freddy yelled, "Need any help?"

"Naw, these kitties have gnawed and scratched the ropes loose." Captain Smith raised himself out of the pit and made a bee line for Ratcliff.

John Smith was madder than a hornet. "Now hear this, you bunch of ignorant ingrates. Get back to work farming and building. I'm in charge and don't forget it.

.

Anyone who doesn't work will be sent back to England when Captain Newport arrives with the first supply and you'll be hung for treason."

## CHAPTER 26
## THE FIRST SUPPLY

**January 2, 1608**

"Ahoy!" Dactyle shouted gazing through an eyeglass. "There be a ship on the horizon."

Freddy took the eyeglass from Dactyle and ran to John Smith. "Captain, I think there's a ship coming."

Captain Smith grabbed the eyeglass. "Blow me down, the first supply is here! You're going to get your ale tonight, mates!"

Captain Newport arrived with the two ships, *John* and *Francis* carrying fresh supplies along with 100 new settlers, two of whom were women. Arriving with the men were Mrs. Forrest and her maid Anne Burrus, who was soon to be married to Thomas Layton.

Seeing the miserable plight of the thirty-eight men left and the situation at the camp, Captain Newport called a meeting. "What happened since I saw you last?"

Ratcliff was the first to speak, "Sir, Captain Smith deserted us. We had no food or defense. He should be hanged for deserting his men."

Newport said, "What say you, Smith?"

"That's a boldfaced lie." Captain Smith pulled out his knife, ready to fight. "It is true, sir, that I left the fort on a mission to trade and befriend the savages. I managed to gain the trust and support of the great Emperor Powhatan. After I left, the leadership here disintegrated." Captain Smith pointed at Ratcliff shouting, "That rogue is not even who he says he is. His real name is John Sicklemore. So who are we to believe?" Smith spit his words out. "Wingfield is now under house arrest. Captain Kendall was convicted of conspiracy and shot. Bunch of dim wits."

Captain Smith led the group to the provisions he had brought. "When I arrived today with these gifts of turkey, venison, corn and these vegetables from the Great Emperor Powhatan, these nutters tried to hang me."

"Well, it's no use crying about the past. Let bygones be bygones. Put your knife away, Smith. We have one hundred new settlers eager to work and build a new country...two of our settlers are women. Mistress Forrest has come to Jamestowne to join her husband and she brought Anne Burrus, her personal maid. Treat these ladies with respect," Captain Newport said.

\*\*\*\*\*\*

"FIRE! FIRE! FIRE! The fort is burning!"

Everyone ran inside the fort to witness a fire that was engulfing the colony's first church. Freddy ran toward the blazing inferno. As he reached inside his pocket and rubbed the Quell Stone, he felt the familiar sensation that had brought him to Jamestowne so long ago.

"Come, Freddy, come! Come, Freddy, come!" Red and orange heat surrounded him. He was being propelled into the diabolical firestorm and through a tiny chamber no larger than the head of a pin. He saw his mother and tried to reach her. He heard her comforting words. "Freddy you are strong and able to make wise choices. Never give up. Never, ever give up."

A strong, swirling wind pulled him through the chamber. The light! The blinding white light had the sound of a roaring tornado. It pulled Freddy through its pin-sized center. Freddy was free falling and spinning out of control. Then, silence.

Deathly silence.

# CHAPTER 27
# FREDDY BECOMES A CHUKKA

"**O**kay, Freddy! Your time's up. Come on out. You're now an official Chukka!" Eustace was blowing the whistle like it was the fourth of July.

No sound or movement came from the initiation room. "Fredaroni! Come on out! The initiation's over!" Duzak yelled.

Silence.

The boys looked at each other showing signs of worry. "Whadda you think's goin on?" Jesse said.

Concerned, Tony said, "Maybe he died of fright. I know I don't have the guts to go in there again."

The boys began yelling, "Freddy! FREDDY! FREDDY! Stop kidding around, man." No response.

Eustace began blowing the whistle again and marching in circles.

Tony ventured into the initiation room. On the far side of the room he could make out a figure in the fetal position. As he neared the figure he saw that it was Freddy. Tony bent down. "Freddy, are you all right?"

Freddy began to move and then sat up. "Hey Tony what's going on, man?"

"You're a Chukka, dude! You stayed in this dungeon for three minutes."

"I did? It seems like I've been gone for months. I don't know what happened in here but it was weird." Freddy tried to stand but his legs were rubbery and he felt disoriented and dizzy. He glanced down at his dirty pants and noticed something red sticking out of the top.

"What the…"? He said as he pulled his windbreaker out.

Tony asked, "How'd your jacket get in your pants"?

"Man, I don't know. This initiation was too weird. I went through some kind of force field, landed on a ship going to Jamestowne and had to hide my jacket so the captain wouldn't throw me overboard."

Tony said, "I knew it. This place is haunted. I bet you were kidnapped by aliens,"

"Tony, listen! I went to another dimension and met Captain John Smith and the great Emperor Powhatan. I even played a cool game with some Indian kids and met a brave named Kitchi. I know it sounds unbelievable but it really happened."

Tony gave Freddy a hand up. Freddy's legs felt wobbly and unsteady. As they reached the other guys, Duzak said, "What took you so long? I thought maybe you got snatched up by one of the ghosts Bart is always talkin' about."

Freddy was discombobulated and what he said didn't make sense to the other guys. "The initiation was incredible. I met King Powhatan and smoked a peace pipe and I helped build the fort at Jamestowne. Some of the Indians were fierce and killed so many of our men…."

The guys looked at each other. Duzak was the first to speak. "Freddy, I wouldn't tell anyone about this dream you had. It sounds cool and all, but you probably hit your head and knocked yourself out. I wouldn't want anyone to think you've been smokin' something."

"Dusak, this was real. I don't care what you think," Freddy mumbled.

"Meow, Meow." A black cat with white paws poked its head around the corner of the initiation room and quickly disappeared back into the room."

Freddy gasped, "That looks like the kitty I had at Jamestowne. Wait a sec, guys, I've got to see something." Freddy coaxed the little fur ball out of the initiation room.

Freddy lifted it up and examined its paws—seven digits. "Oh my gosh!" Freddy said, "I'm taking this cat home."

The boiler suddenly fired up, sending plumes of steam and sounds of howling bellows from within its mighty furnace. "Oh for Chris's sake!" yelled Duzak.

"What's wrong?" asked Eustace.

"I just messed my pants."

"You what?" they all said in unison.

"It was that stupid boiler. I thought I had to fart. Listen, no one must ever know about this. I mean it, dudes."

"Hey, your secret is good with us," Jesse said. "Right guys?"

Eustace held his nose and said, "Oh, man, what's that stink?"

"It's Duzak, stupid."

Eustace began blowing the whistle again and marching in circles.

"Cut it out, bugle boy." Duzak yelled.

"Hey, come on!" Freddy said, "We'd better get back to the Rex or my butt is gonna be on fire."

Duzak said, "Freddy we ain't taking that cat in my car."

"No, look, guys, this is a special cat…It's got seven toes. It's supposed to bring good luck."

"Oh yeah, right. Who ever heard of a cat with seven toes?" Jesse said.

"What are you? The information police?" Tony quipped.

"It just so happens that I read all about seven-toed cats while I was doing research for my Jamestowne report. Come on, Duzak. We won't be in the car that long," Freddy said as he held the little kitten to his chest.

"Sorry Charlie," Dusak said, "not in my *Merc*. Cats don't like to ride in cars….he'll be fighting and clawing everyone trying to get out. I just got my seats done. No way!"

"Duzak, listen, all I have to do is wrap him up in my jacket. I'll hold onto him real tight and he'll be alright. Trust me. I've done this a million times," pleaded Freddy.

Duzak finally gave in. "O.K. Frederoni, this one time, but it's on your head if anything gets messed up."

Jesse howled, "Duzak, I think you've already messed up. Pee-yew!"

Suddenly, Tony realized his friend looked like he had just been shot out of a canon. "Guys! Look at Freddy! What happened to you, dude?"

Duzak said, "What's that on your face and in your hair?

Jesse said, "Yuck!  You're all oiled up like a greased pig."

"That's what I've been trying to tell you.  I was on the ship the *Susan Constant* and met Captain John Smith, who's a real cool dude, and he made me put all this gunk on so the guys on the ship wouldn't get suspicious and throw me overboard."

Duzak shook his head, "You're so full of it."

Freddie yelled, "What time is it?  If I'm late I'm gonna be in BIG trouble."

"Don't sweat it.  We've got ten minutes to get back," Duzak said.  "Let's blow this joint.  Last one out has to wash my shorts."

Duzak covered his driver's side seat with about ten red rags he had stored in the trunk of *The Merc*. He handed Freddy a bunch and told him to clean up.

Eustace rode front middle; Jesse was riding shotgun.  Eddie, Freddy and Tony were in the back.  Freddy had his little black kitty wrapped in his windbreaker; it was purring and closed his eyes. Freddy leaned down and whispered, "Boots?"

"What'd you say about boots?"  Eddie asked.

"Oh I was just wondering when I was going to get my boots…you know, my Chukkas."

"I'd say right away, lover boy. You gonna be hangin' with us you gotta have the right stuff. CHUKKAS!" Duzak screamed at the top of his lungs.

It was exactly ten o'clock when *The Merc* slid into the parking lot of the Rex. The rat rod was already there. Freddy didn't see Charles.

"Quick, let me out," Freddy said, pushing on the front seat.

"Hold your horses, man. Stay cool," Jesse yelled. As soon as Jesse opened the door Freddy was already squeezing over Eustace and out of the car. Freddy went over to the curb, sat down holding his red bundle.

"There you are," Charles said sounding a bit annoyed. "I've been looking all over for you. Kids said they hadn't seen you for about thirty minutes. Where you been?

"I just came out for some air and this little kitty came up to me. It was shivering and looked hungry. I just couldn't help but pick him up and try to get him warm." Freddy unwrapped the kitten and handed him to Charles.

"Oh look, he's got white paws, like he's wearing socks," Charles said. "Freddy! Look at his paws. He's got seven toes. I've heard something about seven-toed cats being good luck."

Freddy said, "I've named him Boots. I want to keep him."

"Hold on there, buddy. I don't know what I am going to do about you. You know good and well your grandmother won't let any fur bearing animals in the house."

"Well, couldn't he stay down in the basement with you for a while? He won't be any trouble and I bet he's a good ratter."

"He is kinda cute. It's cool how he has seven toes. I guess we could try it… But wait a minute…how come you smell like smoke, huh?"

"Charles, I can't help it if some of the guys smoke cigarettes. It's really disgusting and makes me sick to my stomach just to smell 'um."

Charles took a hard look at Freddy. "How come your undershirt is filthy? What's with your hair? Okay, Freddy. You better tell me the truth."

"Well," Freddy said trying to think of something. "I did go for a ride in *The Merc* and it overheated. So I got under the car to see if oil was leaking. The under carriage was oily and gunky. Black stuff got all over me. I know I shouldn't have gone for a ride with Duzak but the guys started poking fun at me ....calling me chicken. I guess I just wanted to fit in."

Charles stared at Freddy for a while. Then he shook his head and laughed. "Freddy, I don't believe a word of what you just told me. I'm just awful glad you're back safe and sound."

Freddy hung his head.

Charles let out a big sigh. "Okay, I guess I need to get you home."

Freddy wrapped Boots in his jacket and got in the car.

# Chapter 28
# Thanksgiving

The following school day was the last before the break and also the performance of the Thanksgiving Musical.

It was a huge success. After the applause and excitement, Freddy finally felt he belonged. He knew he had to go on living and make his mother proud. He also wanted to show more appreciation towards his Gran-dama. Freddy realized that it had been a tough adjustment for everyone.

Freddy's last hour of the day was English with Miss Scales. When the students were settled in their seats after the musical, she picked up a book titled *Great Poetic Songs of Our Time*. She opened the book and turned to a dog-eared page.

"The lyrics to most songs are none other than poetry set to music. This is precisely why I wanted to point out the inferior poetic quality of the song Francis exposed us to today. It goes something like this…..

*"I found my thr-ill*
*On blueberry h-ill*

*On blueberry h-ill*
*When I found you*
*The moon stood st-ill*
*On blueberry h-ill*
*And lingered un-til*
*My dreams came true.*

"However I do notice an AAAB rhyme scheme." Miss Scales took a handkerchief out of her pocket and wiped her nose.

She glanced at the book *Great Poetic Songs of Our Time*, sighed and then cleared her throat. With closed eyes she inhaled deeply. She began to recite Carl Sandburg's *Chicago* with a lusty, primal voice.

*"Hog Butcher for the World,*
*Tool Maker, Stacker of Wheat,*
*Player with Railroads,*
*and the Nation's Freight Handler;*
*Stormy, husky, brawling,*
*City of the Big Shoulders:*
*They tell me you are wicked and I believe them,*
*For I have seen your painted women*
*under the gas lamps luring the farm boys..."*

By the end, Miss Scales was practically hyperventilating.

"This poem has character, passion, and life." She closed the book, turned and placed her hand over her heart.

Freddy raised his hand. "Miss Scales, I know *Blueberry Hill* may not be the best poetry in your estimation but it was written in 1940 and Glenn Miller's Band used to play it."

"Don't you think I know that? I was just trying to make a point." She tilted her head thoughtfully for a moment. "Actually I rather enjoyed the Thanksgiving Musical. I hope everyone has a splendid holiday and remember to work on your historical essays."

Miss Scales went to the front closet to freshen up and put on her hat.

\*\*\*\*\*\*

Mrs. McVicker turned off her alarm, and looked at the clock.

5:30 a.m.

"Well, I guess I'll get up." She yawned and stretched. "No use hurrying. There won't be any festivities around here this Thanksgiving."

Dressed for the day, Mrs. Mack padded down the back stairs to the kitchen. She heard clattering and clanging. Mrs. Mack peered around the corner.

232

"Mrs. Webbe, you're a sight for sore eyes. Can I help you?"

"Ellafaire, I can't find anything...haven't been down here in so long." Mrs. Webbe was dressed in a blue and green plaid skirt, white silk blouse with a turkey broach at the collar. Her hair was pinned up in a French twist and her face was fully made up. "Do we still have any of those Thanksgiving aprons around here?"

"Yes, I keep them in a drawer in the pantry. Do you want one?"

"I don't want to get my clothes all dirty fixing dinner." Mrs. Webbe was opening cabinets, rummaging around, "Where's the big roaster?"

Mrs. Mack came back with a fall colored apron and helped Mrs.Webbe slip it on. "What are you doing?" Mrs. Mack said.

"Well, first of all I need to stop feeling sorry for myself and start living again. I have my grandson to think about now. I have so much to be thankful for so I want to start by cooking up a great big Thanksgiving feast."

A big smile covered Mrs. McVicker's face. "Oh, this is a good day. Are you sure you're up to it?"

"I feel better than I've felt in a long time. So where's the turkey? We've got to get that bird trussed up and baking if we plan on eating by one o'clock."

Soon the kitchen was buzzing with activity. Potatoes were peeled, the crust for the pumpkin pie was rolled out, and cornbread stuffing made. The delicious smell of Thanksgiving dinner wafted throughout the house.

Charles popped into the kitchen at eight o'clock for his first cup of coffee. He was startled to see Mrs. Webbe in the kitchen setting the place on fire with her activity. "Oh, excuse me," Charles said, backing out the door.

"That's all right, Charles. Come in and have your coffee," Mrs. Webbe said. A dab of flour streaked her nose and cheek. "Sit down."

"Okay, if you insist."

"Cooking makes me feel alive...I used to do a lot of holiday cooking before Mr. Webbe, you know...left. We had some happy days."

Mrs. Webbe gazed out the window. She brushed back stray curls from her forehead. "Anyway, Charles do you have plans for today?"

"This evening I was going over to my sister's for a little get together."

"Will you eat Thanksgiving dinner with us this afternoon then...around one?"

"That's very generous of you, Ma'am. I'll look forward to it." Charles put his empty cup in the sink. "Well, I guess I'll see you later, then."

Mrs. Webbe called out, "Oh, and Charles— wear something comfortable." She returned to stirring the batter for the pumpkin pie.

Mrs. Webbe and Mrs. McVicker chatted on. Mrs. Webbe wanted advice on what Freddy would like for Christmas. They talked about redecorating Freddy's room. Mrs. Webbe became animated talking about Christmas, decorating Eagle's Nest and shopping for presents.

At ten o'clock Freddy entered the kitchen. "Grandama! What are you doing in here?"

"Come give me a hug, Francis." She kissed him on the forehead. "To answer your question, I am cooking. Today's Thanksgiving! We're planning on eating at one o'clock in the formal dining room. Charles is going to join us."

Freddy ate a piece of toast and gulped down some milk. "I guess I'll go hang out with Charles," he said. Freddy was amazed. *I wonder what's come over Grandama?*

******

Mrs. Webbe, Freddy, Charles and Mrs. McVicker gathered outside the dining room for a few moments before Mrs. Webbe slid back the huge oak door revealing the beautifully set table, sparkling with glass goblets and fine china. The golden brown turkey was set at the head of the table. Mrs. Webbe indicated for Charles to sit where he could carve the turkey.

"We're liable to have a big mess on our hands if I have anything to do with this bird. Are you sure you want me to do this?" Charles chuckled.

Mrs. McVicker tied a white canvas apron around Charles. He took the silver meat fork and stuck it deep into the breast meat. He cut a thick slice of white meat from the bone. "Anyone want this hunk of turkey? "

"Just cut me off a drumstick," said Freddy.

The meal was delicious by everyone's account. Freddy got dibs on both turkey legs and had seconds on mashed potatoes and cornbread stuffing. It was such a beautiful day that Mrs. Webbe suggested they eat dessert on the veranda.

The maple trees were blazing in crimson glory. The mums, in full bloom, filled the yard with splashes of purple, orange and white. It was quiet, except for the last song of the cicadas. Freddy and Charles talked about racing cars while Mrs. Mack and Gran-dama strolled the yard, picking off heads of withered flowers.

The day was perfect.

## CHAPTER 29
## CHRISTMAS TIME

On December first, Charles and Freddy went to Tavin's Hardware Store in hopes of finding the perfect Christmas tree. There in a corner Freddy spotted "the one." It was a ten-foot blue spruce. After paying a whopping $30 dollars, Charles strapped the tree to the top of the limo.

"Want to get some hot chocolate at the Rex?" Charles asked.

"Oh yeah!" Freddy patted his stomach and licked his lips.

They were sitting in a booth sipping steaming cups of hot chocolate when Charles nudged Freddy and pointed to the cosmetic counter. "Hey Freddy, someone's making eyes at you…"

Freddy turned to see a vision of heavenly splendor. His heart started racing and his knees felt weak. It was Carly. He quickly picked up a menu and hid behind it.

"Charles, that girl gave me her phone number the other night and I haven't called her. I'm gonna pretend I don't see her."

"That's not a good plan," Charles said.

"But I'm sure she hates me by now," replied Freddy.

"Oh, really? I don't think so, Einstein. You've got to step up to the plate and put this girl out of her misery."

"You're not making any sense, Charles."

"Use your head. You need to buy your Gran-dama a present, don't you? Just casually stroll over to the counter, start looking around, pretend you've just seen her and then ask her for advice on a nice present for your grandmother. Now, you're going to have to take it from there. If you lose this one, I can't help you."

"I can't do it"

"Why?"

"My hands are sweaty."

Freddy's heart was beating so hard it hurt. He took a deep breath, sauntered over to the cosmetic counter and stared at the perfume. Rivers of perspiration were rolling down his armpits.

"Freddy...hi! What are you doing?" Carly smiled.

"I was just trying to decide what kind of perfume to get my grandmother."

"You're looking at Old Spice. That's for men."

"Right. Could you give me a suggestion? I don't know what ladies like." Freddy wiped his hands on his jeans.

"I'm really in kind of a hurry. You can ask the saleslady to help you."

Suddenly as though he had no control over his tongue, Freddy began talking really fast. "Carly, I'm sorry I haven't called you. I wanted to but every time I picked up the phone to dial your number I just kept hanging up. Once I actually did let the phone ring but when you answered I hung up."

"Oh, so you're the mystery caller."

"Uh... I was...uh..." Freddy's tongue felt swollen and unmanageable.

Carly looked at him. He realized her eyes were iridescent green, like emeralds. She touched his arm. "What is it? You can tell me."

"Well I was wondering if you're going to the New Year's Eve Cotillion. My grandmother said I have to go...there's no way out for me."

"Why yes, Freddy, I do plan to go. I love dressing up and using good manners." She assumed a proper voice. "Yes, Mr. Griswold, I would love some punch, thank you," Carly giggled. "Have you been practicing your fox trot?"

"I think mine's more like a fox squat," he replied.

"I'm sure it's fabulous!" Carly said clapping her hands.

"So, I guess I'll see you there? By the way, Miss Archer, do you think I could have the first dance?" Freddy ventured.

"Most certainly, Mr. Griswold, I would be delighted."

Carly gave Freddy a pinch on his arm. "Uh, oh, there's my mom. I have to get going. Sorry I couldn't help with the perfume. Tah, tah."

Freddy thought his knees might buckle before he got back to the booth.

"So does she hate you?" Charles was grinning from ear to ear.

"She's saving the first dance for me at the Cotillion Ball. Oh boy, I hope I get my sweaty palms under control before then."

\*\*\*\*\*\*

Charles drove carefully all the way to Eagle's Nest. The limo drew quite a few stares as it passed by with the big spruce tied on top.

The tree was brought into the house and set up in the foyer by the stairs. It looked perfect. Gran-dama selected her favorite holiday albums and stacked them on the spindle of her record player, to drop down and play automatically. The house was filled with Christmas music.

Charles brought the Christmas tree decorations down from the attic. Gran-dama, Charles, Mrs. Mack, and Freddy spent the better part of the day putting the ornaments on the tree, drinking hot mulled cider and singing Christmas carols. Finally the moment came to plug it in.

Glorious! Spectacular! Breathtaking!

They all sat and stared at the tree, reflecting and breathing in the aroma of Christmas. *I wish Mama was here to see this.*

"I'm getting a bit tired. I think I'll recline in the study before I pack it in for the night," Gran-dama said.

"Gran-dama, I have something I've been wanting to ask you."

"Let's go into the study." Gran-dama said.

Freddy pulled up a side chair next to his grandmother.

There was a long pause like all the air was being sucked out of the room. Freddy's stomach tightened at the possibility of the answer.

"Well, what do you want to talk about? I hope it's not some boy thing I know nothing about. That's what Charles is for."

Another pause. Freddy inhaled. "Who's Miguel?"

"I don't know what you mean? Why are you asking?"

Freddy went over to Grandama's desk, pulled out her address book and returned to sit by his grandmother. Freddy opened the book and pulled out the picture. He pointed. "This guy right here with his arm around Mama. On the back it says Miguel. So, who's Miguel?"

Mrs. Webbe cleared her throat. A rip of panic hit her. "Oh Lord, help me. I never thought this would come out." Grandama looked to the heavens.

"Oh, Freddy, I've been so stupid. I've done things I'm not proud of. If only we could go back in time" Grandama said her voice quivering. "I only hope you can forgive me for what I'm about to say."

Freddy stared at his grandmother, waiting.

"First, let me say this. Things were different back then. We had all these rules. A person couldn't associate with someone out of their race or social standing. It just wasn't done."

Freddy said, "Is he my father?"

Mrs. Webbe squeezed and twisted her handkerchief. She looked at her hands. "Yes."

"Were you ever going to tell me?"

Gran-dama stuttered, "I don't know. It just never seemed like the right time."

"Well, I think the right time is now," Freddy said. "Start at the beginning and tell me all about my father."

"I think the beginning was when Miguel called your mom and invited her to his Senior Prom. He attended St. Anthony's Academy. He was the Prom King. He wanted your mother to be his date. Hannah told him she'd call him back because she had to get my permission."

"Hannah approached me so excited and told me Miguel Griswaldo had invited her to his prom and could she go?"

"Freddy, you have to understand that in the 40's, white girls only went out with white boys." It wouldn't matter if his father was the president of Mexico. Miguel was a Mexican and she wasn't allowed to go out with him. Hannah cried and pleaded, locked herself in her room. I could hear her wailing and sensed her pain but I wouldn't budge." Mrs. Webbe grabbed a tissue. Her eyes welled.

"Little did I know she began sneaking out to see him. Then, she finally seemed to calm down. On the night of the prom she went to the movies with John Harrington—

good family; his ancestors date back to Jamestowne. I didn't know it but Hannah and John were in cahoots. He picked her up and took her to a girlfriend's house where she changed into her prom dress. After the prom, Hannah and Miguel sneaked across the river and got married in Mexico. This was all to be kept a secret until after graduation."

Freddy was listening with great intensity. He was bewildered. *Why would you keep two people who loved each other apart?*

"Eventually this kind of secret begins to show. One evening I pulled Hannah aside and asked her right out if she was with child. She said yes and confessed that she and Miguel were married."

"I went berserk. How could she ruin our family name like this? It sickened me. I literally dragged her up the stairs and into your room. I slammed the door and told her this marriage was going to be annulled. I confided in Mrs. McVicker and we decided to tell everyone that she had gone to live with an aunt in Kansas. Right before you were to be born, Hannah returned to St. Wigbod."

"I called on Mrs. McVicker. She had been a midwife before coming to work for us. Ellafair tended to everything I guess it took about 30 minutes for you to be born. Hannah was so happy just gazing at you. After about a week, Miguel showed up at our door requesting to see his son. Oh, the nerve!"

"I told him he could see you this one time but it would have to be out on the veranda. Hannah came down with little baby Francis. That's when the photo was taken."

"He kept calling you his little Francisco and saying how you'd be a great caballero one day. When he left I thought, 'Good riddance to bad rubbish.' Your mother kept herself locked in her room and said she wouldn't come out until she could see Miguel again."

"About two months later one of Hannah's school chums stopped by the house. He asked if he could take Hannah out for a ride. I thought she was strong enough and Mrs. McVicker said she'd watch over you."

"It was eight o'clock. I'll never forget the time. The emergency room at our hospital called to say there had been a terrible accident and Hannah had been thrown out of the car but she was stable. The driver had died at the scene."

"I rushed to Hannah's side. She was barely conscious. Hannah kept repeating over and over, Miguel, Miguel, Miguel!"

"That's when I realized the scheme they had hatched up. Hannah's friend from school picked her up so she could be with Miguel."

"When I tried to say something to Hannah she turned her face to the wall."

"Freddy, I've been so wrong on so many things. I just hope you can forgive me. I love you so much. We live in a different world now." Gran-dama reached out for Freddy's hand and squeezed it. "I would like to make up for all the grief I've caused. I want to live to see you graduate and get married and have lots of grandchildren."

Freddy put is arms around Gran-dama and buried his head on her shoulder."I love you, too. I guess we have each other now Gran-dama." Then he added, "Where are my father's parents?"

# CHAPTER 30
## COTILLION

It was two days before the 'Big Event'. Tony and Freddy made plans to go to the cotillion together. Charles said he would take them in the limo. Duzak and Jesse wouldn't be attending because they had been caught doing doughnuts in the parking lot of the school and Mister Hister suspended them for a week. Their parents grounded both boys for the whole Christmas vacation and Duzak's parents took his driving privileges away until further notice.

Mrs. Wingfield's School of Manner's and Courtly Conduct was sponsoring the cotillion at the St. Wigbod Country Club. Those lucky enough to have been invited spent weeks practicing social graces, table manners and ballroom dancing. The dress code was strictly enforced.

Properly dressed St. Wigbod teenagers began arriving at the Country Club by eight o'clock on New Year's Eve. The foyer of the country club was elegantly appointed. Grand chandeliers laden with Austrian crystals hung from the ceiling. Thick oriental carpets graced the polished hardwood floors.

| _Girls:_ | _Boys:_ |
|---|---|
| Party dress | Dress shirt and tie |
| Tights or nylon stockings | Dress slacks |
| White Gloves | Black belt |
| Dress shoes, white or blue | Black shoes, black socks |
| Clutch purse | Jacket or suit |

The smooth sound of Les Brown and His Band of Renown could be heard floating from the ballroom. A gigantic crystal ball was turning in the ballroom producing shimmering, swirling specks of lights. A few couples were already dancing but most of the invitees were milling around the refreshment tables.

Charles pulled up under the canopy at the country club at ten minutes after eight. Tony and Freddy jumped out of the limo and bounded up the steps to the receiving hall. As soon as Freddy entered the hall he began looking for Carly. Tony hit up the refreshment table. Erin wobbled in wearing green high heels to match her gown. Her red hair was in a French twist; tiny ringlets framed her face.

Freddy ambled over to her "Hey, Erin. Have you seen Carly?"

"What am I—chopped liver?" Erin twisted her pearl necklace, wiped her teeth for lipstick and adjusted the top of her strapless gown. "I hope this thing stays put."

"Oh, I'm sorry. What I meant to say was, Miss Frith, you look absolutely divine. Would you care for a cup of punch?" Freddy made a low bow.

"Why yes, Mr. Griswold. Thank you very much."

Pointing to the refreshment table Freddy said, "Tony's piggin' out on the shrimp. You should go talk to him."

Freddy returned from the punch table sloshing pink liquid with each step. He froze when he saw Carly chatting with Erin. *Slow down, don't slip in punch.*

"Here you go ladies," Freddy handed Erin and Carly each a cup.

Carly looked enchanting. Her shimmering red taffeta dress was set off perfectly by dangling rhinestone earrings and a matching necklace. She wore red satin shoes. A white gardenia held one side of her hair back, away from her face. Eyeliner made her green eyes pop. Freddy thought she must be a goddess.

"First dance?" Freddy asked.

.

"Why yes. I believe I do owe you the first dance," Carly said placing her cup on a table.

Erin wandered over to the refreshment table and edged up to Tony. "You're sure eating a lot. Mama said that good manners dictate one should not stuff up like a turkey at Cotillion. Mixing all that food will turn your gills green. I know. I drank too much eggnog Christmas Eve and spent the whole night hugging the toilet."

Tony wadded up a pimento cheese sandwich and gulped it down. "This is the only reason I came," his voice garbled by an over-filled mouth.

"Want to dance?" Erin asked.

"N-n-n-o. I don't feel so g-g-good." Tony felt his stomach churning. He ran off holding his hand over his mouth.

Erin was disappointed. *Oh great! Now I won't get to dance.* She crossed her arms and looked at the punch table. John Stevenson was pouring something into the punch bowl from a small flask. Quickly he screwed the cap on and put it in his pants' pocket.

Erin marched over. In her teacher voice she said, "What are you doing?"

"What?" John looked around the room for chaperones. "Beat it, skinny bones."

"You put alcohol in the punch, didn't you?"

.

"This place needs to loosen up."

"I'm gonna tell if you don't ask me to dance." Erin stared at John her mouth pursed.

John weighed his options, looked at the floor and mumbled, "Wanna, dance?"

Erin offered her white gloved hand to John and they ambled off to the ballroom.

Around the floor of the grand ballroom, tables were set for ten. China dinnerware, glass goblets, silverware, and cloth napkins folded into origami swans were at each place. The salad plates were already out. At each place were a New Year's Eve hat, noise maker, paper streamers, and confetti. The ballroom was aglow with glitz and sparkle.

The band finished its first set. Mrs. Wingfield approached the microphone. Her shrill, quaky voice announced, "Ladies and Gentlemen of St. Wigbod, welcome to our New Year's Eve Cotillion. Everyone looks beautiful..." she snort-laughed. "Of course I'm referring to the ladies...you boys look good, too."

There was mild whistling before she shushed them. "Mind your Cotillion manners. Now, for a few details... I want to recognize and thank the many teachers who so kindly agreed to chaperone tonight's event." These chaperones were standing along the sides of the room  and

Freddy noticed Miss Scales and Mr. Gore standing together. "We will dine at this time. Name cards have been set out indicating where you will sit. Gentlemen, assist the ladies at your table. Use the table manners and etiquette we have been practicing. After dinner, gentlemen, you will escort the lady on your right to the dance floor for the bunny hop. Bon appétit!"

There was general confusion as boys and girls searched for their place cards. Students at each table were from different schools to encourage mingling and making new acquaintances.

Freddy found his place and stood waiting for the rest of the table to arrive. A cute blonde girl wearing a rose colored gown with a sequined bodice found her place next to Freddy. Soon ten teenagers were standing around the table. Freddy took the initiative, pulled out the chair for the cute blonde next to him, and the other boys followed suit.

Greetings and introductions followed. Freddy found himself at a table with two girls from Ratcliffe, a couple of guys from St Anthony's Academy and the others were from public schools. The swan napkins were unfolded and placed on their laps. There was quiet chattering about which fork to use for the salad and who was to pass the rolls.

The entre was served: Glazed chicken with wine and mushroom sauce, mashed potatoes pressed onto the plate to look like a flower, and green beans almandine.

Freddy attacked the chicken first. With a fork in one hand and a knife in the other he began cutting. His fork slipped and the whole chicken breast, sauce and all, slid into his lap.

"Nice work," a boy from St. Anthony laughed.

Everyone at the table laughed and the girl next to Freddy said, "Don't worry. It happens to me all the time."

Freddy picked the chicken up with his hands and put it back on his plate. In a quaking voice Freddy mimicked Mrs. Wakefield. "There will be no eating from your lap." He snorted. "Bon appétit!"

This broke the table up in fits of laughter causing other tables to look over in disapproval. This was the ice breaker they needed.

Freddy learned his dinner partner was named Candy Newport, an eighth grader at Ratcliffe. She boarded because her parents lived on a ranch in a remote part of the state. She said that at times it was lonely, but you get used to it. Freddy told Candy a little about himself, about his accident and the loss of his mother. He confided he was getting used to living with his grandmother.

Freddy felt a tap on his shoulder. Someone was whispering in his ear.

"What are you doing over here? You should be at your own table," Freddy said.

Giggling, Erin declared, "I drank some of the punch."

"So?"

"John spiked it. I saw him. I feel sooo funny." Erin began to sway. Freddy scooted his chair back and caught her before her knees buckled.

"Oh, this is not good. Let me get you back to your table."

"I don't want to. I want to sit here, with you," Erin slurred. "I love you. I've had a crush on you ever since I ran into you the first day of school."

"I've got to get you some fresh air and coffee," Freddy said holding onto her arm.

"Can I help"? Candy said. "I think she needs to go to the powder room."

"Yeah, that's a good idea."

Freddy and Candy each grabbed Erin around the waist and tried to walk her to the bathroom without arousing any suspicions from the chaperones.

The two girls disappeared into the powder room while Freddy stood watch outside. Candy came out with a report.

"She's thrown up once and is still hugging the pot. Be back with more details," she reported.

Miss Scales and Mr. Gore strolled dangerously close to the powder room. They eyed Freddy with suspicion and each gave him that 'We know you are up to something look.'

Freddy wiped his sweaty palms on his trousers. He could see Principal Hister at the punch bowl, dipping the ladle into the brew. *Oh, no, this dance is going to be over before it really gets started. Stupid John.*

The powder room door opened. Candy was holding Erin by the waist as though they were best friends. Erin's ringlets were dangling, wet and gooey. Her mascara streaked down her cheeks, she was pale, and smelled like vomit.

"Are you feeling better?" Freddy tried to act concerned.

"Oh Lord. I never want to drink anything stronger than a Coke ever again. Mama told me that liquor is the wrath of grapes," Erin lamented.

"We need to get back. People at your table are going to start wondering where you are. Candy, do you have any gum or something to tone down her smell?"

"Yeah. In my purse. I'll get you fixed up."

Freddy escorted Erin back to her table, pulled out her chair, leaned over and whispered. "This is our little secret. No one has to know."

Erin looked up and feebly nodded her head. "Thanks, Freddy." Then she looked around at her surprised tablemates and said, "Everyone having a good time?"

The band leader took the microphone. "Everybody up! It's time for the Bunny Hop. Escort your dinner partner to the floor and let's have some hoppin' good fun."

Out on the dance floor, the students formed a line, the music blasted, and soon the whole group, including chaperones, was hop, hop, hopping. The band went right into *Earth Angel*. An awkward moment followed. Couples seemed uneasy, not knowing what to do, and looking around.

"Would you like to dance"? Freddy asked. "I'm kind of sweaty from The Bunny Hop."

"Why yes," Candy smiled.

Freddy held her in the appropriate dance position and the two glided around the room. They passed Carly dancing with some guy he didn't know. When the song ended Freddy and Candy made their way over to Carly and her partner. Carly introduced Tommy Sands from St. Anthony's.

"When the next song comes up, why don't we change partners," Freddy suggested.

"That's a good idea," Carly agreed and winked at Freddy.

"Here's another romantic classic, *You Send Me*," the band leader announced.

Freddy pulled Carly close, his hand connected to the small of her back and he lead her around the floor. They danced past Miss Scales and Mr. Gore who nodded. "It looks like we may have a little hokey pokey goin' on," Carly whispered. Freddy laughed.

The Twist was next in the lineup. Let's go get something to drink. I'm bone dry," Freddy said.

There was a commotion at the refreshment table. Mrs. Wingfield was all a flutter. "Oh, dear! This punch has been spiked. Don't anyone have another drink from this punchbowl." Waiters came and took the liquored-up bowl away. "You'll just have to drink water from now on." Mrs. Wingfield's voice rose an octave higher.

The final incident of the evening occurred when John Stevenson was caught throwing cherry tarts out of the second story window at people on the sidewalk below. His parents were called and he was escorted out by Coach Beast. Mrs. Wingfield followed behind scolding and lecturing him.

Les Brown announced the last dance, *Goodnight, Sweetheart.* Freddy was caught up watching John's ejection from Cotillion. When he turned to look for Carly, he saw Bobby Ford asking her to dance. *Oh well, you snooze, you lose.*

Abruptly the song ended, the lights came on and Mrs. Wingfield took the microphone. "It's midnight. Everyone get your hats and noise makers. Happy 1958!"

The band played *Auld Lang Syne,* noise makers blasted, confetti flew, streamers sailed high, landing on the happy revelers. Some gave kisses; others looked for a place to hide. Many escaped to the restrooms. Freddy found Carly throwing streamers with Erin. He took some of her streamers and wrapped them around her shoulders. "This really has been a great time. Happy New Year!" He looked into her eyes.

"Happy New Year, Freddy." Carly stood on her tiptoes and gave Freddy a kiss on the cheek.

The song ended and Les Brown announced that the dance was over. Suddenly there was a scramble to get coats, find rides, and say goodbyes.

Tony appeared disheveled. "What happened to you?" Freddy asked.

"It's a long story. I don't want to talk about it."

Erin piped up, "He got sick and threw up. He missed the whole dance. I told him not to stuff himself but he wouldn't listen."

"You're one to talk. Put a sock in it, Erin." Freddy said.

Carly was the first to be picked up. From the back seat of her parent's 1958 red Buick, she rolled down the window, waved at Freddy and yelled, "I had a really great time!"

A lonely sadness welled up in Freddy. It hit him in the pit of his stomach. "I wonder what's happening to me? I feel sick."

Standing alone under the awning Freddy noticed Erin. He strolled over to his friend, a whiff of vomit still lingering. Erin stared straight ahead, her arms hugging her waist.

"Fun time, huh?" Freddy said.

Erin's shoulders drooped. "For you."

Freddy shuffled his feet and put his hands in his pockets. "It's okay, Erin. No one knows. This kind of thing happens to everyone at some time or another."

Erin covered her face with her hands. "That's easy for you to say. You didn't just puke your guts out at the Cotillion. Look at me. My dress is ruined, my hair is matted with upchuck. My mother is going to be so disappointed in me."

Freddy chuckled, "And you're going to have one hell of a hangover tomorrow." Freddy fished in his jacket pocket and produced a small notebook and pen. I'd like to give you a call...to see how you're doing. Here, jot down your number."

Erin looked at Freddy. "I wish I was like you... Not a care in the world and so cool."

Freddy blushed and said, "You're my best bud, Erin. I hope we'll always be friends."

A white 1958 Chrysler 300 pulled around the drive. "There're my parents. Thanks for the pep talk." Erin looked back at Freddy. "You've got my number." She mouthed, "Call me."

# CHAPTER 31
# THE NEED FOR SPEED

S pring time in St. Wigbod was coming in like a lion. The wind storms were kicking up and making Freddy and his friends antsy to get outdoors and enjoy the warmer weather. At a meeting in Duzak's garage, The Chukka's talked about making their group into an official car club—The Chukka Car Club—CCC. Most all the racing in town had been along country roads and the police had been breaking up their fun saying it was too dangerous and someone was going to get hurt or killed.

"What we need is a drag strip," Duzak complained.

"Fat chance of that happening," Jesse said. He handed Duzak a wrench.

"Fredaroni, hey! What about talking to Charles or your grandmother about a strip? I heard she used to race around like a wildcat back in her day," Duzak said.

"How would that help?" Freddy said.

"She's in all these clubs and stuff. Maybe they do projects to help kids have something to do." Duzak said. "My dad is always saying that we need a raceway to keep us off the streets."

"Well, I could ask."

Charles picked Freddy up at five o'clock that Saturday afternoon. Freddy hopped into the bomber seat; the engine revved up, and Charles made a burnout.

"Charles, where do you race?"

"Usually we meet at the old dry reservoir east of town. Not really that great…but we can test out our cars and get a sense of how fast they'll go." Charles had his elbow on the window ledge. "Want to go out there and open her up?"

"I'd love to but Gran-dama said I have to give a presentation at the Jamestowne Society meeting tonight…read my report. Maybe tomorrow, huh?"

"We'll see."

******

The limo left Eagle's Nest at seven o'clock. Gran-dama was wearing a black suit with a red flowered pin on

262

the lapel; Freddy was in his school uniform. He fidgeted and twisted his report into a cylinder.

"Freddy, stop rolling your report like that. You won't even be able to read it. Besides it's beginning to look like something the dog dragged in." Gran-dama took the report from Freddy and smoothed it out and then she got her compact out. She checked her lipstick and powdered her nose.

"Gran-dama, does the Jamestowne Society ever sponsor any projects to help the community or young people?"

"Sometimes. Why do you ask?"

"Well, you know, I'm in the Chukka Car Club. Um...well...the guys don't have any place to race and we got to talkin' today. What we need is a drag strip... so that we could race in a safe place. I've been reading in *Hot Rod* that a lot of innovations for the automobile industry are coming from drag strips...like the one in Big Spring."

"You know what? I heard some of the men at the meeting the other night talking about this very thing. We have quite a few members that like to work on their old cars and soup 'em up. After you present your report I'll bring it up when we get to new business." Gran-dama reached over and tried in vain to get Freddy's rooster tail to

263

lie down. "You got that rooster tail from my father's branch of our family tree."

Freddy smiled.

The Jamestowne Society meeting started promptly at seven-thirty with dinner. Governor Adele Webbe stood and clinked her spoon on her glass at eight o'clock. "Ladies and gentlemen...members of the St. Wigbod Company of the Jamestowne Society. I now call the meeting to order. We are privileged tonight to have my grandson, Francis, present his research report on Jamestowne."

Mrs. Webbe beamed and began the clapping. Freddy went to the podium and tested the microphone. He swallowed hard and then began. "The expedition to found a new colony in the new world had a very perilous beginning...."

At the end of his report the audience gave Freddy a standing ovation.

"Excellent report, Francis. You really uncovered some little known facts. If I didn't know better I'd say you had been there." Governor Webbe said.

"Now we will move on to new business. My grandson is, as are many of his friends, very interested in the mechanics of cars. I'm sure you've seen the hot rod my driver Charles has created." Mrs. Webbe lifted her head with the pride. "I would like to entertain discussion on the feasibility of our group taking on a project to provide a place for the young people of St Wigbod to race their cars and test their innovations."

Lively discussion followed. Capt. William Unger, stationed at Johnson Air Force Base, made a motion and it was seconded that, "A Drag Strip for St. Wigbod be adopted as their group's project of the month."

******

Less than thirty-five days later St. Wigbod had a full-fledged drag event backed by most of the city's civic organizations. The site chosen for the drag strip was the old shut-down airstrip outside of town. All the local citizenry came together to get it ready. The lanes were painted, the pits sectioned off, some cast off risers were brought out for seating, and portable potties hauled over by Dixon Hardware. An announcer's booth was constructed and fitted with a microphone and loud speakers. The first race was scheduled for Friday, the first of May. Price of admission: Fifty cents.

A week before the opening of the drag strip, Freddy found Charles in the garage checking the timing belt on his car. "Are you ready for this weekend?" Freddy asked him.

"I've really got to thrash. I've been waiting on Willy Tankard to do the stenciling and flames," Charles answered.

"What are you going to name this beast?" Freddy got in behind the wheel pretending he was speed shifting.

"I like *Rampage.* What'd you think?

"I like it. Charles, did you talk to Gran-dama about me riding out to the drags with you?"

At just that moment, Mrs. Webbe entered the garage. She stepped over some oil cans. "Oh Francis, there you are. I just finished talking to Miss Scales. She said your presentation on Jamestowne was the best she had ever heard. Sooooo, I know you are dying to go to the races with Charles. As a reward for all your hard work I've decided to let you go."

"Sweet!" Freddy yelled. He ran over to Gran-dama, grabbed her by the waist and swung her around.

Giggling and squirming she said, "Put me down! I swear you are just like your grandfather— always joking around." Gran-dama took on a serious demeanor. "Just because you get to go this time doesn't mean you have a free pass. Your grades and behavior have to warrant it."

# Chapter 32
# The Drags

At two o'clock Friday afternoon, Charles and Freddy fired up *Rampage* and headed out to the new St. Wigbod Drag Strip. The trip took twenty minutes. The smell of smokin' tires, burnouts, dust and loud noise filled Freddy with excitement.

There was a line waiting to enter the pits. Freddy spotted *The Merc* and the Conestoga up ahead. Charles revved *Rampage*. VAROOM BA-BA!

Eddie Brinto and his dad directed the cars to parking spaces. The drivers lined up their cars side by side. There was lots of thrashing going on before the races got started. Whole families were working on their cars, groups of boys were adjusting and discussing the setup, while others were cleaning the tires and tuning their engines.

The spectators started showing up about four o'clock with folding chairs and ice chests, setting up along the sides of the track.

A meeting of all drivers was called to discuss the rules and procedures:

1. Two cars would line up, rev their engines and, from a standing start, accelerate for a quarter mile.

2. The flagman would give the signal to start.

3. The losing racer in each heat would be eliminated and the winning racers would progress until one remained.

4. In prestaging, water could be poured on the lane and the driver could make a burnout to get traction.

At four-thirty, the first two cars lined up in their lane in the staging area. Jesse Houlgrave was driving the Conestoga. A senior from St Anthony's Academy was in a 1933 Willys Coupe. The flagman stood between the two cars, pointed his flag at each driver to get set. The flag flew up and the race was on.

The Willys shot away leaving Jesse in the dust. The Conestoga actually did a burnout as Jesse left late. The most Jesse's lead- sled could do was 58 mph. The first heat was won by Ellis Kingston in his Willys. Jesse was eliminated.

All kinds of cars were being raced that night from '35 Fords to Daddy's farm truck to homemade hot rods. . If it had wheels and an engine it could race.

"Big Daddy" Croft brought his portable refreshment wagon. He was selling RC Cola, Coke, popcorn and hot dogs.

He probably made a whopping thirty dollars that night.

\*\*\*\*\*\*

"Come on Ellafaire. Did you get the sandwiches and water?" Gran-dama left the kitchen going to the car. She had a scarf holding her hair back and wore rolled up blue jeans, a white untucked shirt and white tennis shoes.

Mrs. Mack was holding a picnic basket. Wearing dark blue pedal-pushers and a one-size-fits-all flowered blouse, she got into the front seat of the limo and heaved herself down with a huff.

"Do you remember how to drive this big car?" Mrs. Mack said.

"Of course I do, Ellafaire. It's like riding a bicycle; you never forget. Now let's see, where are we going?" Mrs. Webbe laughed.

They followed the highway out of town to the old runway. At least a mile away the noise from the strip could be heard. "I think we've found it." Gran-dama pointed.

She maneuvered the limo up as close to the starting line as possible and parked. "We'll get a good view from here and if you want we can sit on the hood. Ellafaire, look! There's Freddy."

She rolled down the window and yelled out, "Yoo-hoo, Freddy."

*Oh my gosh! I'm just not believing this.* He headed over to the limo and stuck his head in. "I didn't know you were a racing fan." He smiled.

"I do have a little wager on *Ramage* to win."

"Okay, we'll do what we can. I'd better get back. Charles is lining up." Freddy ran back to the pits.

Mrs. Webbe got out of the car to stretch. She spotted several people from the Jamestowne Society sitting in folding chairs. She waved and then heaved herself up on the hood.

"Hurry up Ellafaire! I see Charles in the lineup."

Charles was next. He got the left lane. A souped-up Nash Rambler was on the right. Freddy wet down the track. After a couple of burnouts to warm up the tires, Charles was ready.

The stage was set; the flag man pointed and up the flag went. Charles was late leaving when his tires spun but they caught and then he exploded down the track. The Rambler popped its clutch and stalled out. Charles won.

All night Charles had been winning his heats and now there were just two cars left to run each other— *Rampage* and *The Merc.* The two cars lined up; Charles drew the left lane again. He glanced over at *The Merc.* Duzak gave him a salute. The stage was set; the flagman pointed at each car and up the flag flew. *The Merc* shot off first. Half-way down the track it was a dead heat, they were neck in neck and then *Rampage* edged ahead by a fender. *Rampage* won! The crowd went wild.

Back in the pits people gathered around *Rampage,* looking at the engine, and asking Charles questions about his car. Freddy soaked up the winning feeling.

Duzak and Jesse shuffled up. "Good race, man." They shook hands. "Next time, I'll see you in my rearview mirror." Duzak smiled.

******

Charles and Freddy got back to Eagle's Nest at eight o'clock that night. Freddy was carrying the trophy.

"Meow." Surprised by the sound, Charles looked around.

"Freddy, I think Boots is out. Here Bootsy, Bootsy," Charles called.

Freddy spotted Boots under a bush. "He must have been out all night. Look how he's shivering."

Charles reached under the bush and pulled him out. Boots purred as Charles rubbed him under the chin.

"Charles, let's take him in and see what Gran-dama's reaction is."

"Well I guess this is as good a time as ever."

Freddy entered the kitchen holding the trophy and set it "slap dab" in the middle of the table. Charles was holding Boots like it was as normal as apple pie. Suddenly Mrs. Mack and Gran-dama marched in the kitchen blowing party horns and singing *For He's a Jolly Good Fellow*.

"Freddy, you and Charles make a pretty good team," Gran-dama said. "I guess I know where you two will be on the weekends."

"Yeah, me too. I wonder if I can drive *Rampage* sometime."

"I don't know," Charles said, "I guess that's up to your grandmother."

"I'll have to think about that." Then Gran-dama spotted Boots. "What on earth do you have there?" She stepped over to Charles and scrutinized the kitten. "Can I hold him?"

"Sure," Charles said. "Check out his paws. They look deformed."

"Oh my goodness! I can't believe it. It's a Hemmingway. I've heard of them but never seen one...Ernest Hemmingway collects these kitties at his place in Key West."

Freddy's grandmother petted and stroked Boots. "Where did you find him?"

"He was outside when we got here...Charles heard him crying. Do you think we could keep him?" Freddy said.

"Definitely. This is a very rare breed. But we'll have to keep him inside." Gran-dama was scratching him under the chin.

"I've got a perfect name for him...Boots." Freddy said.

"Bootsy, Wootsy. Ellafaire, get some warm milk for our wittle Boots." Gran-dama watched while Boots lapped up the milk.

Freddy had never seen this side of his grandmother. He was astonished at the effect Boots was having on her.

"Can he sleep with me?" Freddy said.

Gran-dama was kissing the kitty, and holding him up in the air like a baby. "Tonight, I think I'd like some company. Oh, I can't wait to tell everyone I've got a Hemmingway." Gran-dama yawned. "If you don't mind, I think I'll take Boots and head on to bed. This has been a long day." She went over to her grandson and kissed him on the cheek, "Freddy, I am real proud of you." She hugged him tightly. "Well, goodnight all."

"Don't let the bedbugs bite," Freddy said.

Freddy watched as his grandmother disappeared from view. "If you don't mind I'm going to make a phone call." He fished in his pocket and pulled out a rumpled paper with seven digits neatly penned in the center. He whistled as he left the kitchen thinking about the excitement and love he had felt tonight and in spite of all that had happened since last summer he was looking forward to the days ahead.

# EPILOGUE
## THE REUNION

I decided to go to my 50th class reunion, after all. So much time had passed and I wanted to see my classmates and have more left in my life than dreams and memories. After graduating from high school, I went to MacLane University and then on to Webbe Medical School. My grandmother donated heavily to make Webbe Hospital into a teaching facility, specializing in head trauma injuries. The state, then, funded the medical school in St. Wigbod.

I met my wife Sara while in med school and after graduation we settled in the metropolitan area of Cowper, about three hundred miles east of St. Wigbod. Gran-dama passed away at the ripe old age of ninety-two and so I rarely return to St. Wigbod. As per her instructions, Eagle's Nest was donated to the St. Wigbod Historical Society. My beloved Sara was killed in an automobile accident on her way to a medical conference. Despair and loneliness drove me to shut out the world and throw all my energy into work. Two months ago, in an impulsive moment, I stopped by the Chevy House and test drove a new Camaro. I was in love!

I pulled into the parking lot of the St. Wigbod Country Club as nervous as a school boy on his first date. The parking lot was about half full. Everything looked so familiar— nothing much had changed. A knot in my stomach reminded me that I was still that shy kid with the sweaty palms.

There were three older ladies at the registration desk. One gray-haired lady wearing a black suit, sported a spiky hairdo, lots of blush, and dripping in diamonds. She looked me up and down and said, "Okay, Okay, don't tell me. You are either Bobby Ford or Freddy."

I smiled and actually blushed. "I'm Freddy." The three ladies screamed at the top of their lungs. "I knew it!"

They descended on me jumping up and down and screeching like banshees. "Freddy, it's so good to see you. Wow! You are so handsome. Turn around so we can see your butt."

I was laughing so hard. "Wait a sec. At least tell me who you are."

The lady with the spike stuck out her chest so I could see her class picture and name—Anne Dixon. Then I recognized Molly Martin and Kendall Waller from their class picture.

Kendall had gained at least fifty pounds and she said she was fixing to have a knee replacement. Molly really looked about the same only fifty years older.

I got my badge and headed for the bar. I was hoping to see Carly. I quickly downed a scotch and water and felt less anxious.

Two guys ambled up to the bar and checked out my nametag. "Fredaroni!" It was Eustace and Edgar.

We hugged and began talking about old times. They said Duzak went to Vietnam, got into drugs, and messed up his head. No one had seen him in quite a while but they heard he was living in a shelter. Edgar said Carly has MS, is in a wheelchair and rarely goes out.

I felt my heart sink.

"Has anyone seen, Erin?" I said.

"Oh yeah! Man, is she a knockout. Va-Va-Voom." Eustace said. "There she is talking to the principal of Wiggins, Dr. Boangeres.

"Oh, wow! I knew his father."

I sauntered over and waited for a break in the conversation. Erin turned to look at me. Her eyes lit up, a big smile spread across her face and her gorgeous auburn hair shimmered in the light.

"Freddy Griswold! Where have you been all my life?"

"It's so good to see you. You look wonderful."
Freddy was in awe. *Why didn't I notice you in school?*

"Freddy, I'd like to introduce you to Dr. Paul Boangeres, the new principal of Wiggins."

We greeted and I told him I had known his father but as it turned out Bo was his grandfather. He said his grandfather had been active in civil rights and had marched to Washington D.C. with Dr. Martin Luther King Jr. in August of 1963. We chatted politely and finally I asked Erin if she would like to dance.

The night was filled with talk of times long past and old friends. At last I got the courage to ask Erin if she would like to go for a ride in my new car.

As we pulled out of the driveway and onto Country Club Lane, I floor-boarded the car and burned rubber to the end of the block. I could see Erin laughing and thought that after all these years we might discover a new and different relationship. We headed out toward the river like a couple of giddy teenagers.

# Author's Note

The town of St. Wigbod is completely fictional but the story of the beginning of Jamestowne is based upon the journal of Captain John Smith, *The Generall Historie of Virginia, New England & The Summer Isles*. The members of the first crew to reach Jamestowne in 1607 are listed below.

The names in bold indicate characters in the story who could have been descendants of the Jamestowne colonists. My hope is that you were entertained and at the same time learned about America's historical beginning.

## Council:

**Captain Christopher Newport**

**Mr. Edward Maria Wingfield**

**Captain Bartholomew Gosnoll**

**Captain John Smith**

**Captain John Ratliffe**

**Captain John Martin**

**Captain George Kendall**

## Gentlemen:

Robert Hunt, Preacher

Mr. George Percie

Anthony Gosnoll

**George Flower**

**Capt Gabriell Archer**

Robert Fenton

**Robert Ford**

William Bruster

**Edward Harrington**

**Dru Pickhouse**

Thomas Jacob

John Brookes

Ellis Kingston

**Thomas Sands**

**Benjamin Beast**

Thomas Mouton

**Eustace Clovill**

Stephen Halthrop

**Kellam Throgmorton**

Edward Morish

Nathaniell Powell

Edward Browne

Robert Behethland

John Penington

Jeremy Alicock

George Walker

**Thomas Studley**

Richard Crofts

**Nicholas Houlgrave**

**Thomas Webbe**

**John Waller**

John Short

**William Tankard**

William Smethes

**Francis Snarsbrough**

Richard Simons

Edwrd Brookes

**Richard Dixon**

**John Martin**

Roger Cooke

**Anthony Gosnold**

**Tho:Wotton, Chirurg**

**John Stevenson**

Thomas Gore

Henry Adling

Francis Midwinter

**Richard** **Frith**

## CARPENTERS:

William Laxon

Edward Pising

Thomas Emry

Robert Small

## LABOURERS:

John Laydon

William Cassen

George Cassen

Thomas Cassen

William Rodes

William White

Old Edward

**Henry Tavin**

George Goulding

John Dods

William Johnson

William Unger

James Read, Blacksmith

**Jonas Profit, Sailer**

Tho: Cowper, Barber

Will: Garret, Bricklayer

**Edward Brinto, Mason**

William Love, Taylor

Nic: Scot, Drum

Wil: Wilkinson, Chirurg

**Samuell Collier, boy**

**Nat. Pecock, boy**

James Brumfield, boy

Richard Mutton, boy

Divers to equal 106

## Acknowledgements

I have so many to thank for making this book a reality. Bud, thank you, for reading, rereading and helping me with the technical details about drag racing. Thank you Lindsay. You are an amazing editor and idea person, and artist. Holly, your encouragement and love have meant so much. My editor, Barbara De Santis took my words and made them work so much better. A million thanks to my friends Marian Tatum and Barbara Clawson who edited and encouraged me all the way through. I am blessed and beholden to my family and friends. You are my lamps in the world.

Polydactyl Cat

282

Made in the USA
Columbia, SC
02 February 2020